THE
CARING
COOK

*Cruelty-Free Cooking
for Beginners*

THE CARING COOK

Cruelty-Free Cooking for Beginners

JANET HUNT

The Vegan Society
Oxford

First published September 1987 by The Vegan
Society Ltd., 33-35 George Street, Oxford OX1
2AY.

© Janet Hunt

ISBN 0-907337-12-0

Design by Kate Bowen and Craig Wilkinson.

Printed and bound in Great Britain by K & SC
(Printers) Ltd., Tunbridge Wells, Kent.

Contents

Introduction

People's reasons for wanting to follow a cruelty-free, i.e. vegan way of eating (and of life) can vary enormously. Some are concerned about animals and the way in which they are exploited in the production of *all* animal-derived foods (including the wide range of dairy foods that seem so innocent); others will have the ecology of the planet in mind, aware that Western eating habits are destroying the natural balance, killing the soil and, in the process, causing millions to starve in the less affluent and exploited Third World countries.

Many are now becoming vegan for health reasons. With the recent reports of a number of distinguished committees has come a greater awareness of the health benefits of a sound vegan diet. Once upon a time vegans were considered to be cranks, and decidedly unhealthy ones at that, but now nutritionists advise us to cut out, or at least restrict, our intake of animal fats of all kinds. A vegan diet is at last being recognized as desirable rather than dangerous.

The growing swing to this way of eating has generated an enthusiastic response on the part of manufacturers, large and small. There are now alternatives to many of the animal-derived staples — meat, milk, yoghurt, and so on. Though not strictly necessary, these can be a great help to those who have the desire to give up such foods, yet find that they miss flavours and textures that they've known all their lives. (And as these products are completely free from animal ingredients, why not?)

There are also many vegan convenience foods — tins and packets of all sorts of items that will help you vary your diet, as well as save time on those occasions when you really haven't a minute to spare. Not to be relied on all the time, of course, but it's certainly worth keeping a supply of your favourites on hand. *The Cruelty-Free Shopper* — a best-selling and annually revised checklist of 100% animal-free products — and the 'Shoparound' column of The Vegan magazine, listing newly-launched vegan products, are invaluable in this connection.

1

The Balanced Diet

A lot has been written about the importance of balancing your diet if you want to stay fit and healthy. Some say you should combine foods carefully. Others that you should eat only before or after certain times. Others again maintain that you shouldn't touch certain foods and should eat others three times a day. Ideas change so frequently it's sometimes hard to keep up! Ultimately it seems most sensible to aim for just one thing: variety. Other points to bear in mind: fresh foods are better than processed, and raw foods are better than cooked (think of the time this will save you in the kitchen). We probably don't need as much protein as the 'experts' used to think, but we do need some (nuts, grains, tofu, TVP, anything made from soya beans — all these are excellent sources).

If you've been a 'meat 'n two veg' person you'd do well to rethink your whole approach to meals, as well as to what you eat at mealtime. You can, of course, just substitute a non-animal protein for the meat you would have eaten, but there are other, far more interesting, ways of preparing and serving food. Take a look at the recipes given in this book and others — especially those with recipes from other cultures. Cooking is, or should be, a creative art. Imagine the ingredients to be like a paint palette. Mix them and use them to create new dishes and different effects. Put unlikely ingredients together and make a note of the results. Use spices and herbs to add interest. Throw out the rules along with the meat, and have fun in the kitchen!

Entertaining

What better way to convince others of the wisdom of your ways than to invite them for a meal? When doing this first decide what kind of meal is going to have the most appeal to *them*, not you. An obvious, but often overlooked point! If your guests are conventional, they'll probably prefer a 'normal'-type meal, maybe with a meat substitute in a sauce of some kind — i.e. 'sensible' food that will prove you're still relatively normal and will not totally disorientate them or their tastebuds. Others may jump at an opportunity to try something new and exotic that shows that vegan food can be every bit as exciting as any other food, and doesn't need to rely on ingredients like mock meat!

Once you've decided on your approach, choose your recipes. (If you're planning something special and haven't cooked it before, do try to have a test run — dinner parties are NOT the time for experimenting.) Apart from the recipes given here, there are numerous other books available (many direct from the Vegan Society) offering culinary ideas, plain and fancy, to suit all tastes.

Plan and prepare your meal, set an attractive table and then relax and enjoy yourself.

Get Set, Go!

Some people switch from being carnivores to vegans literally over-night. They make up their minds, and that's that. Others do it one step at a time — generally cutting out meat and fish first, then moving on to eggs and dairy produce.

Whichever category you belong to, good vegan eating starts with setting up your kitchen. This doesn't necessarily mean going out and spending a fortune on high-tech equipment (though you can, of course, if you like). What it does mean is planning to make the best use of the space you have, providing at least the most basic tools for the job, and organizing storage. Three lists follow suggesting the items you'll need, and some extras you might like to indulge in! You may well already have most if not all of them. Remember, it's worth buying better-quality kitchen equipment — it will do the job better and quicker, and if looked after carefully will last a lifetime.

Vital

• A set, or at least a couple, of heavy saucepans with well-fitting lids. They should be of different sizes. Enamelled iron or cast-iron are best. Stainless steel is also a good choice.
• Two sharp knives — one large, one small. Get the very best you can afford as they're prime tools in the kitchen.
• A grater (for nuts, fruit, making crumbs).
• A steamer — the fold-up stainless-steel kind are ideal as they fit most saucepans.
• A wooden spoon (gentle on the pots!).
• A spatula.
• A tablespoon.
• A measuring jug. (Plastic will do, but Pyrex is better.)
• A mixing bowl.
• A board for chopping things on — also useful for kneading dough. (Plastic-coated will do, but hardwood is best.)

- A rolling pin.
- A colander.
- A wide-necked thermos flask, in which you can leave beans, rice, soups etc. to cook all day — so your food is ready when you are.
- An oven-to-table dish — for casseroles, crumbles — that kind of thing.
- Cooking tins and trays — one baking sheet and one small loaf tin at the very least.
- A flan ring (stand it on a baking sheet when making flans).
- A small fridge.
- Storage jars of various sizes. These can be purpose-bought or old sweet or jam jars can be pressed into service. Make sure the top fits properly to exclude air — and dark or opaque materials are better than clear, as light can leach goodness out of foods.
- A plastic box for sandwiches or whatever you might wish to take as part of a packed lunch.

Useful

- An oven-to-table flan dish.
- More cooking tins — a small loaf tin for nut roasts etc., a larger one for bread, a swiss roll tin, etc.
- A wire whisk for sauces, etc.
- A small grinder, electric or hand-operated. Invaluable for powdering nuts, grains, beans, seeds etc. Some of the electric ones have a blender attachment so you can also purée vegetables and fruit.
- Skewers. Use them for vegetable kebabs (or for speeding things up when baking jacket potatoes).
- A fridge plus small freezer.
- A sprouter for making your own bean and grain sprouts for half the cost of the shop-bought variety. Inexpensive and simple to use.

Luxury

- A wok. If you like stir-fried vegetables, there's no better way to cook them. It isn't necessary to buy the most expensive, but choose one that's heavy and well made.
- A pressure cooker (preferably stainless-steel) will cut the time needed to cook all those beans, not to mention other things!
- A pasta-making machine. For those who like to make their own pasta dough (it's easy — and nothing compares with it for taste) and want to be able to serve it in a variety of shapes.

4

Now all that remains to do is to stock up with ingredients. Vegans are lucky in that many of the foods that are basics in a meatless diet will keep very well. If you've space you can save time and money by buying things in bulk — beans, wholegrains, tahini, dried fruits etc. Store these in a dry, dark place, preferably in an airtight container. Nuts and seeds, vegetables and fruit, and flours such as wholemeal and soya need to be bought in smaller amounts as they tend to go off quickly. Tins and packets can, of course, be used to supplement fresh foods — keep a supply in and you'll never be caught out.

Go through the following list and see what you need to buy for your store cupboard and fridge. Some of the ingredients you may well be able to do without, especially if you cook only occasionally and are not interested in anything but the quickest to prepare and most basic of meals! But anyone wanting to be adventurous in the kitchen would do well to collect as wide a range of ingredients as possible. Buy in small amounts to start with, and use carefully the first time — how many first attempts have been disastrous enough to put someone off a food for life?!

Do also keep an eye open for all the new vegan foods coming onto the market, whether via traditional outlets — whole- and health-food shops — or, increasingly, your local supermarkets and delicatessen. Refer regularly to *The Cruelty-Free Shopper* and 'Shoparound', and if you like the sound of a certain product, but can't find anywhere that sells it, encourage stockists to supply it by asking them to — more than once, if necessary.

For your store cupboard

Agar-agar. Obtained from certain seaweeds, this colourless powder is an excellent alternative to gelatine. Use two teaspoonfuls to set a pint of liquid. It's particularly good with acid fruits.

Carob. If chocolate doesn't agree with you use carob instead. It tastes much the same but contains no caffeine, and is unlikely to cause allergic reactions. The powder is ideal for cooking and in drinks. Carob bars can be melted to give biscuits a delicious coating, or grated to sprinkle over dessert dishes.

Fruit. Both fresh and dried fruits are full of nutrients (not to mention fibre) and should be included in everyone's diet. Try to vary them. Fresh fruit in season is better food value than the artificially grown varieties, though if you can afford it the occasional indulgence in imported strawberries or whatever can liven up the most mundane meal. Buy a variety of dried fruits and keep in airtight containers. Use them in desserts, breakfast cereals, as a quick snack, and in savoury dishes too — they're lovely with salads.

Grains. These are the seeds or seedlike fruit of cereal grasses and are packed with goodness. Although rice is one of the most popular, don't forget the others — millet, wheat berries, bulgur (cracked and partially cooked wheat), barley, corn, rye, buckwheat (not strictly a grain but used as one). Oats have the highest protein content of all — use them in crumbles, to thicken soups, and to make cakes with.

Herbs. These make food more interesting and easier to digest, contain vitamins and minerals, and have various medicinal qualities. Try to grow at least a few in the garden, or in pots on the window ledge. If dried is the best you can do, use half the amount — as they're much more concentrated.

Milk substitutes. Usually derived from soya beans, these vary enormously in texture and taste, ranging from the downright unpalatable to the delicious. You may, therefore, have to experiment before settling on one that's just right for you. They come in three forms: powdered (great when you don't use much — so can make up just what you want when you need it — and easy to store); ready-to-use (mostly in long-life packs); and concentrated (you add water as needed, though you can use them just as they are — super on fruit salads, puddings etc).

Nuts & seeds. One of the most concentrated forms of protein available, and a good source of fibre, vitamins and minerals, nuts are a real wonder food. They're also easy to store (in small amounts in an airtight container), very versatile, and delicious to eat. Though some of them are expensive, you only need to use small amounts, so do try other varieties besides the ever popular peanut! Seeds such as pumpkin, sunflower and sesame are also worth discovering.

Pasta. Made from finely ground wheat, pasta is a basic ingredient with which you can make countless meals. Some pastas have spinach added to give a green colouring. (Some also have egg added — so be sure to read the packet.) Wholemeal pastas are worth getting for the added nutrients and fibre. With pasta in your cupboard, you need never be stuck for a quick and inexpensive meal.

Pulses. The edible seeds of leguminous plants (e.g. peas, beans, lentils) and a staple food around the world. They are inexpensive, will keep for ages if stored in a cool, dry spot, and offer lots of nutrients. They need to be properly cooked if you don't want trouble digesting them! Soak them for a while first, boil for 10 minutes, then lower the heat and simmer until they are well cooked. Surplus cooked beans can be kept in the fridge until needed.

Soya products. The soya bean is used to provide a huge range of 'alternative' foods, many of which are vegan staples. Soya flour adds protein and can be used as an alternative to eggs for binding cakes, pancakes etc. Soya sauce gives a strong, salty flavour (plus various nutrients) to savoury dishes. Soya mayonnaise is fine as an alternative to the egg-based variety. For other soya products see **Milk substitutes, Tofu, and TVP.**

Spices. Like herbs, these can help make a meal more exotic, can bring out the flavour of ingredients, and are wonderful aids to digestion. Buy a few small packets, store them in dark airtight jars and then experiment. You only need use a pinch of most spices as they're very concentrated.

Sweeteners. Though refined white sugar is no longer (in this country, at least) produced by a method involving animal bones, it is worth paying that little extra for raw cane sugar. The taste is infinitely better and, unlike white sugar, it still contains a few nutrients. Syrup is good for cooking, though this is made from white sugar — except for real maple syrup, which is a completely natural product (expensive, but worth buying and keeping for special occasions). Molasses is highly nutritious and is also the sweetener with the lowest calorie count.

Tahini. This is a thick, whitish paste made from crushed sesame seeds, sometimes with a little sesame oil added. A darker variety is made from roasted sesame seeds and has a stronger flavour. Although it's fairly expensive, a jar goes a long way. Try it in both savoury and sweet dishes, or mix it with a little maple syrup for the most delicious cream substitute ever!

Tofu. A soya bean curd packed with protein and other nutrients, and with a bland taste that makes it ideal for use in both sweet and savoury dishes. It comes in several different varieties, the most widely available of which is firm tofu — best for deep-fried cutlets or use in sauces such as bolognaise. The softer 'silken' tofu is more suitable for making sweet dishes, fruit whips, cheesecake-type flans — that kind of thing. There is also a smoked variety of tofu, which has a distinctive taste and is great fried with other vegetables.

TVP. The initials stand for Textured Vegetable Protein, and refer to the packets of meat-like chunks or mince made from soya or field-beans. While some are flavoured and others are plain, all have a texture similar to that of meat — which means they can be a godsend to those who miss the real thing! Best used in sauces, to make burgers, or as a filling in pies. TVP is not expensive when you consider its high nutritional value, and the fact that the contents of a small packet will expand, when hydrated, to feed a whole family.

The Vegan 'Dairy'. For those who miss dairy produce, there is now an increasing range of alternatives — though not all of them taste exactly like the originals. The thing to do is to try them — with interest in vegan food booming, regular additions are coming onto the market, and your chances of finding substitutes for non-vegan favourites are improving daily. In addition to milk and cream substitutes, look out for soya yoghurts and 'ice creams'.

Vegetables. Orthodox eating habits have relegated vegetables to playing a bit part at mealtime. This is a tragedy, since there are now more kinds of vegetables available in our shops than ever before — some home-grown, many imported, and all of them good sources of vitamins, minerals and fibre. Make a point of using vegetables regularly, and imaginatively. Buy them often, keep them in the cool, and use them whilst they're at their best. (Organically-grown varieties are better than those produced with the aid of chemicals. Ask your nearest shop to consider stocking some — potatoes, for example, which are now produced on a large scale.)

Notes to the recipes

Unless otherwise indicated the recipes are for four adults.

Where margarine appears as an ingredient, *vegan* margarine is always implied (see *The Cruelty-Free Shopper* for brand names).

Abbreviations:
g — gram(s);
tbs — tablespoon(s);
tsp — teaspoonful(s);
ml — millilitre(s);
mm — millimetre(s)

Breakfasts

It is said that breakfast is the most important meal of the day. After a long night of fasting, and before a busy day, we all need to refuel. But who has time for the huge breakfasts that have been part of the British tradition for so long? And who — when rushing to catch the bus or train — can digest them?

Certainly it makes sense to eat something after what may be twelve hours, or even more, without food. The important thing is to choose the kind of food you enjoy, that suits your individual metabolism, and that can be prepared without too much fuss. Right now the cereal breakfast is in fashion. Not the cereal breakfast of the seventies — puffs of nothing covered in sugar and drowned in milk. Today's cereals are based on ingredients such as wholegrains, nuts, and dried and fresh fruits. Served with soya milk, they offer all the nutrients you need to get (and keep) you going, yet take next to no time to not only prepare, but to eat too.

You don't like cereals? Fine. Try wholewheat bread spread with nut butter, yeast extract, maple syrup, or low-sugar jam. Or eat American-style and have sweet muffins, doughnuts or scones for breakfast. Providing they're made with wholesome ingredients, they'll do you as much good as a fried breakfast — more in fact! If you don't enjoy eating in the morning, drink your breakfast instead. Mix ground nuts into grapefruit juice, blend tofu with orange juice, soya milk or soya flour with pineapple. If you've got an extractor, make fresh fruit juice — or vegetable if you prefer a savoury taste.

As for those rare occasions when you fancy a traditional breakfast with all the trimmings, why not? Go right ahead. Use vegetable oil for frying, replace meat sausages with the vegan variety (from tin or packet), add mushrooms and tomatoes — and don't forget the toast and marmalade.

Breakfast may be the shortest meal of the day, and the one eaten with the least fuss and ceremony, but that doesn't mean you shouldn't enjoy it!

Tropical Muesli

1lb (455g) mixed cereal base (or a combination of oats, barley and rye flakes)
3 oz (85g) dried apricots or peaches, coarsely chopped
3 oz (85g) dates, coarsely chopped
2 oz (55g) banana chips
4 oz (115g) coconut flakes
good pinch of cinnamon (optional)
2 oz (55g) ground almonds

Put the cereal into a bowl. Stir in the coarsely chopped fruit. Add the banana chips and coconut flakes.

Add the spice and ground almonds, if using them both.

When all the ingredients are well mixed, transfer them to a large airtight container.

Use as needed.

Nice with: Soya milk. Coconut milk would make this muesli even more exotic! An alternative is to put the muesli into a bowl and cover it well with water. Leave overnight. By morning it will be creamy and ready to eat.

Variations: Try dry roasting the coconut flakes first for extra flavour. You could use dried bananas — chopped into small pieces — instead of the crunchier banana chips. You can, of course, use your own choice of nuts and dried or fresh fruit.

Crunchy Malt Granola

1lb (455g) oats
4 oz (115g) walnuts, whole or coarsely chopped
2 oz (55g) almond flakes
4 oz (115g) wheatgerm
2 oz (55g) sesame seeds
2 tbs grated lemon peel
approx. 4 tbs vegetable oil
approx. 4 tbs malt extract
6 oz (170g) raisins or sultanas

In a large bowl mix together the oats, walnuts, almond flakes, wheatgerm, seeds and lemon peel.

In a small bowl stir together the oil and malt extract. Pour this mixture over the dry ingredients and stir again so that everything is lightly coated with the oil. Use a little more oil and/or malt if necessary.

Spread the mixture across a large baking pan (use two if necessary) and bake at 300°F/150°C/Gas Mark 2, stirring frequently, until golden and crunchy.

Take the pan from the oven, let the mixture cool slightly, then stir in the raisins or sultanas. When completely cold store the granola in an airtight container.

Nice with: Soya milk, concentrated for special occasions. Or try it with soya yoghurt for a change.

Variations: Any mixture of nuts can be used. Other grains such as rye or barley flakes can replace some of the oats. Other dried fruits can be added (after cooking, or they may dry out too much). If you don't like the taste of malt, use syrup instead. Although granola is traditionally made in the oven, it can also be cooked in a heavy-based pan on top of the cooker. Always stir frequently.

> When measuring malt extract, syrup, or any sticky substances, oil the spoon first. The substance will just slip off without leaving a trace!

Hot Grain Dish

Put the water into a saucepan, add the *kasha* and salt. Bring to the boil, then lower the heat until it is bubbling and continue to cook gently for about fifteen minutes, stirring every now and again.

The resulting dish is rather like porridge, only with a more definite taste.

> approx. 11/2 pints
> (850ml) water
> 1/2 lb (225g) *kasha*
> (roasted buckwheat)
> pinch of salt

Add water if necessary so that you get the consistency you prefer.

Nice with: This porridge, though highly nutritious, is rather plain. It can be 'livened up' in a number of ways — just before eating, stir in some undiluted soya milk, add sweetening (molasses is unusual), or a few spoonfuls of fruit purée or jam. Sprinkle with nuts or dried fruits.

Variations: This basic cooking technique can be used with most grains — including oats! — to make a hot breakfast dish. Grain flakes cook quicker than whole grains.

Shredded Wheat De Luxe

4 shredded wheat biscuits
2 tbs bran or bran cereal
2 oz (55g) cashew nuts, coarsely chopped
4 oz (115g) dried pears, coarsely chopped
4 oz (115g) prunes, soaked overnight
2 medium bananas
raw cane sugar (optional)

Crumble each of the biscuits into a bowl. Divide the bran, cashew nuts and pears between the four bowls.

The prunes should be plump and soft. (Any cooked prunes left over from a previous meal can be used) Remove the stones, chop the flesh, and share it between the bowls.

Peel and chop the bananas — half a banana for each portion.

Sprinkle with sugar if liked (or hand it round at the table for those who have a sweet tooth!)

Nice with: Creamy soya milk.

Variations: Any dried fruit and nuts can be added to shredded wheat in this way — you can mix up a large amount, store it in an airtight container and have

it ready for use. The stewed and fresh fruit should, of course, be added at the last minute. Also try using other basic commercial cereals — such as Weetabix, Puffed Wheat or Wholewheat Flakes.

Scrambled Tofu on Toast

Mash the well-drained tofu then fry it in the vegetable oil, turning it frequently so that it is evenly cooked.

Add plenty of seasoning and turmeric to give it an 'eggy' colour, as well as to add taste. Chopped chives or parsley look attractive scattered over the top.

Cut the slices of hot toast in half, spread with margarine and put three pieces on each plate. Divide the tofu mixture between them.

If liked, top the mixture with a knob of margarine and extra parsley.

Variations: Instead of serving the tofu on toast, put it on a plate with fried mushrooms, tomatoes and maybe fried bread — and you've got a really traditional breakfast!

**10 oz (285g) tofu
approx. 2 tbs vegetable oil
seasoning to taste
pinch of turmeric
(optional)
chopped chives or parsley
(optional)
6 slices wholemeal toast
margarine**

There are plenty of ready-mixed mueslis in the shops nowadays, but some of them contain milk powder, most of them are over-sweetened, and they're expensive. Mixing your own takes next to no time and means you know exactly what is in it! As it keeps well, providing it is stored in an airtight container, you can make up enough to keep you going for weeks.

Soups and Salads

Strange to say, soups and salads have a lot in common. They make good starters, but can also be a meal in themselves. They can be cool and refreshing in summer, chunky and satisfying on a cold winter's day. (Yes, salads too.) They can be thrown together in minutes, using just a few simple ingredients, or — when you want to impress — they can be true Cordon Vert!

Given that you can now buy an enormous variety of soups in tins, packets and boxes, it's not surprising that few people bother to make their own. But it's a shame. There's nothing to compare with home-made soup, and it really needn't take much longer than opening a packet. Throw a few vegetables and cooked beans (left-over or tinned) in with some stock — add pasta or cooked grains for a thick or filling soup. With a side salad and bread, you've got a well-balanced meal. If you've got a blender (well worth investing in if you like soups) you can purée left-overs in literally seconds, add herbs or yeast extract, and simply heat the soup through. (Or serve it chilled, with a spoonful of soya yoghurt or tahini stirred in for a creamy texture.)

If you're having soup before a main course, be sure to balance it up — don't make it too heavy (it should stimulate the appetite, not dull it), and base it on different ingredients from those being served later.

The making of salads is your chance to be really creative. Go for colour and effect as well as taste. Choose the freshest ingredients only (though you can always add a few cooked items — such as sweetcorn — for interest, and cold vegetable dishes like ratatouille make excellent salads when served on a bed of lettuce.) Easy in summer, you may say, but what about when there aren't many fresh salad ingredients to use? Use vegetables. Raw leeks, brussels and parsnips, for example, are lovely finely grated and used in not too large amounts. Add them to a rice salad with nuts, a creamy dressing — and you've got a complete meal in a salad bowl! (And don't forget bean and grain sprouts — easy to grow at home, inexpensive, nutritious and delicious . . . the perfect all-year-round salad ingredient.)

Cauliflower Soup with Walnuts

1 medium cauliflower
1 oz (30g) margarine
1 onion, finely chopped
2 tbs wholemeal flour
13/4 pints (1 litre)
    vegetable stock
seasoning to taste
good pinch of nutmeg
    (optional)
2-3 tbs concentrated soya
    milk (optional)
2 oz (55g) walnuts,
    coarsely chopped

Trim the tough outer leaves from the cauliflower, cut off the stalks, and divid the florets into small sections.

Melt the margarine in a saucepan and fry the onion until it begins to soften. Add the flour, stir and cook briefly

Pour in the vegetable stock and bring to the boil, so that the sauce thicl ens. Add the cauliflower florets, cover the saucepan and cook over a low heat for about 20 minutes.

Purée the mixture in a blender, add seasoning and nutmeg and return the soup to the saucepan. Heat gently unti hot again. Pour into individual bowls.

For a creamier soup you can stir in drop of undiluted soya milk.

Sprinkle each bowl with nuts.

Curried Leek Soup

4 medium leeks
2 tbs vegetable oil
1-2 tsp curry powder
13/4 pints (1 litre)
    vegetable stock
6 tbs cooked brown rice
seasoning to taste
small piece creamed
    coconut (optional)

Clean the leeks very carefully by makin a slit down the side, then running cold water over them. Slice into thin rings and drain off as much of the water as possible.

Heat the oil and fry the leeks for a few minutes, stirring once or twice. Sprinkle in the curry powder and cook few minutes more.

Add the stock, bring to a boil, then lower the heat and cover the saucepan Continue cooking gently for about 10 minutes, or until the leeks are soft.

Add the rice and cook until heated

hrough. Season to taste.

If used, grate the creamed coconut and stir it into the soup so that it dissolves. Serve at once.

Variations: Any vegetables can be cooked in this recipe — or try a combination. Other left-over grains can take the place of rice, or throw in a handful of split red lentils to add bulk — not too many, though, as they absorb a lot of water and so may turn your soup into a purée!

Creamy Mushroom Soup

Cook the onion gently in the oil for five minutes, stirring frequently. Add the mushrooms and cook for five minutes more.

Pour in the liquid, add seasoning, bring the mixture to a boil, then cover the pan and lower the heat. Simmer for about 15 minutes. Cool briefly.

Blend the mushrooms together with the liquid to make a thin purée and return this to the saucepan.

Mix the water and flour until smooth and paste-like. Add this to the mushroom purée. Heat gently, stirring continually until the soup thickens. Stir in just enough tahini to give the soup a creamy colour. Serve at once.

Add chopped parsley or chives to give both flavour and colour — mushroom soup is rather dull to look at! Croûtons can be handed round at the table — to be sprinkled over the soup by those who want them.

1 small onion, chopped fine
2 tbs vegetable oil
1/2 lb (225g) mushrooms, sliced
13/4 pints (1 litre) vegetable stock or water
seasoning to taste
2 tbs water
1 oz (30g) wholemeal flour
approx. 2 tbs tahini
chopped fresh parsley or chives (optional)
wholemeal croûtons (optional)

Croûtons can be made in minutes, and they really are nice with creamy soups. One way is to toast thin slices of wholemeal bread, then cut them into tiny cubes. You can also cube the bread first then fry gently in oil — turning the cubes frequently, until crisp. Drain them on paper towels before serving. (Some people add a touch of garlic to the oil first for garlic-flavoured croûtons!) They'll keep for a few days if stored in a screw-top jar.

Chestnut Soup

12 oz (340g) chestnuts
1 1/2 pints (850g) vegetable stock or water
1 stick of celery, finely sliced
1 carrot, finely sliced
1 small leek, finely sliced
2 tomatoes, peeled and finely chopped
parsley or other fresh herb
seasoning to taste

Cut a cross in the top of the chestnuts and either bake them in a hot oven for 10 minutes, or boil them in a saucepan of water for about the same time. When cool enough to handle, use a knife to carefully remove the shells and inner skins (it helps to hold them in a kitchen cloth).

Chop the chestnuts coarsely and put into a clean saucepan with the vegetable stock or water, celery, carrot, leek and tomatoes. Bring the liquid to a boil, then lower the heat, cover the pan and cook the contents gently for a further 10 minutes, or until all the ingredients are just cooked.

Stir in fresh herbs, season to taste, and serve at once.

Variations: If liked you can blend the ingredients to make a thick, smooth soup. Instead of herbs, you might like to try a good pinch of grated nutmeg.

To peel fresh tomatoes, put them into a bowl and pour on boiling water. Leave them for a few minutes, during which time the skin will split and begin to curl. Drain the tomatoes, and use a sharp knife to peel them.

Green Lentil Soup

Put the water into a saucepan. Drain the lentils and add them to the fresh water along with the prepared onion, carrots, and celery. Bring the mixture to a boil, reduce the heat, cover the pan and simmer gently for about an hour, or until the lentils are cooked.

Add seasoning, parsley, and a good sprinkling of 'Smokey Snaps', and leave for just a minute. Then serve the soup at once so that it's piping hot.

Variations: Other pulses can be used instead of the lentils — try split peas for example. (Split red lentils make a quick version as they take half the time to cook.) If you prefer, you can purée the mixture in a blender for a smooth soup — add the 'Smokey Snaps' afterwards for texture contrast.

**2 pints (1.15 litre) water
or vegetable stock
6 oz (170g) green lentils,
soaked overnight
1 medium onion, chopped
2 carrots, chopped
2 celery sticks, chopped
1 tsp dried parsley
seasoning to taste
soya 'Smokey Snaps'**

The quickest way to thicken soup is to add a spoonful or two of fine wholemeal breadcrumbs. The quickest way to make it creamy is to stir in some tahini. The quickest way to add protein is to drop in small cubes of tofu a minute or so before the soup is removed from the heat.

19

Tomato and Tofu Soup

2 tbs vegetable oil
1 small onion, finely
chopped
1/2 lb (225g) tomatoes,
peeled and chopped
4 oz (115g) carrots, peeled
and chopped
11/2 pints (850ml)
vegetable stock
2 tbs tomato purée
10 oz (285g) tofu,
well drained
1/2-1 tsp dried oregano
good pinch of paprika
seasoning to taste

Heat the oil in a saucepan and fry the onion for a few minutes. Add the tomatoes, carrots, vegetable stock and tomato purée. Bring to the boil, then lower the heat, cover the pan, and cook gently for 15 minutes. Purée the cooked ingredients plus the tofu in a blender. When thick and smooth, add the oregano, paprika and seasoning. Taste the soup, adjusting the flavouring if necessary.

Reheat gently before serving.

Variations: Also good when chilled. A sprinkling of chopped chives or spring onions adds colour and taste.

Harvest Soup

3 oz (85g) peas
13/4 pints (1 litre) vegetable stock or water
14 oz (395g) tin tomatoes,
coarsely chopped
2 medium potatoes,
scrubbed and cut into
cubes
1 red pepper, sliced
4 oz (115g) green beans,
trimmed and sliced
1 medium onion, chopped
2 oz (55g) wholemeal
spaghetti, broken into
pieces
1/2 tsp yeast extract

In a large saucepan mix together the peas, liquid, tomatoes, potatoes, pepper, green beans and onion.

Bring the mixture to a boil, then cover the pan and lower the heat. Cook for 10 minutes. Add the pasta pieces and cook for 10-12 minutes more, or until all the ingredients are just tender. Flavour with yeast extract, basil and seasoning.

Variations: If fresh peas and green beans are not available, use the frozen kind. Try macaroni or pasta shells for a change from the spaghetti pieces, adding a drop more liquid if necessary.

Salads

Salads have a bad reputation. If they're not seen as little more than a garnish — the colourful bit that goes with the savoury, but certainly isn't there to be eaten! — then they're associated with self-denial, with eating to be thin and/or healthy, but not for pleasure.

In fact, they can be a real treat of flavours and textures; can be a complete meal (if served, for example, with wholemeal baps or a jacket potato), a first course at a special dinner party, and are ideal for summer patio or picnic eating.

The secret is improvisation. Any vegetables can be used in a salad. Most are fine raw, but if you prefer you can lightly cook the tougher varieties such as leeks and parsnips. Fruits can be added, and fruit juice is as good as any dressing! Fresh herbs are delicious chopped and added raw to salads. A sprinkling of nuts, seeds or cooked beans add protein, as well as a crunchy texture — as do plain or garlic croûtons!

The art of dressings isn't so much in the making, as in knowing which dressing goes best with which ingredients. Imagine, for example, a simple cabbage and carrot slaw with thick peanut dressing, or a traditional combination such as lettuce, cucumber and tomato with an exotic curried tofu dressing. Then again, a salad such as one containing beans, raw onion and/or radishes, would benefit from a classic French Dressing to which you've added fennel or ginger to aid digestion. If you're putting dressing onto a large bowl of salad, instead of inviting everyone to add their own, there are two things to remember: do it at the last moment, and add only the minimum amount (the dressing is intended to bring the salad alive — not drown it!).

A few final tips then, before you start making your own salads:
- Always choose the freshest possible ingredients, smaller rather than larger (the longer the vegetable grows, the more likely it is to be tough), and prepare the salad as close as possible to when you plan to eat it.
- Keep in mind the colour, texture, taste and shape, and aim for an interesting mixture.
- Traditionalists suggest a salad should include some green leaves, at least one root vegetable, a crunchy ingredient — such as celery or apple — and a colourful one like red pepper, or a sprinkling of cooked sweetcorn. Having said that, my own personal favourite mix is endive, lettuce, iceberg lettuce, sliced chicory, plus a scattering of watercress — similar ingredients, and all of them green!

Classic French Dressing

**6 tbs vegetable oil (olive or sunflower are best)
3 tbs lemon juice, cider or wine vinegar
seasoning to taste**

If the dressing is to be used at once, put the ingredients into a bowl and whisk so that they are thoroughly blended. If you intend to store them, put them into a small screw-top jar and shake well. Keep this dressing in the fridge and shake it again before using.

Variations: This simple dressing can be adapted in countless ways. Here are a few suggestions to start you off. Once you've got the idea you'll probably come up with plenty more of your own! Simply add the extra ingredients to the basic mixture, and whisk or shake well.

• Add 1/2 clove or more of finely chopped garlic.
• Add a good pinch of curry powder, ginger, cumin or turmeric.
• Add 1/2 tsp of made mustard and chopped fresh herbs.
• Any herbs can be added, either singly or in a mixture — don't overdo it though. Tarragon is considered especially good.
• A sprinkling of soya sauce adds inter-est — you might need to add a little sugar too, as the taste can be rather strong for some people.
• 1/2-1 small onion or a few spring on-ions finely chopped.
• 1-2 tbs sesame seeds.
• 1-2 tbs ground almonds.

And for a thicker French Dressing — just chill it until a few minutes before it's needed. It will be creamier without your needing to do a thing more!

Tofu Dressing

Either mash the tofu well with a fork and then mix with the other ingredients or, better still, put them together into a blender for a much smoother dressing.

Store in the refrigerator for a few days if necessary — though it won't keep for long.

Variations: All the additions suggested for the use with Classic French Dressing can be added to this dressing with different — but no less tasty! — results.

> 6 oz (170g) tofu, well drained
> 2 tbs vegetable oil
> 2 tbs cider or wine vinegar
> seasoning to taste.

Peanut Butter Dressing

In a bowl, stir together the peanut butter, lemon juice and enough water to give the dressing a pouring consistency. Add mustard and seasoning to taste.

This dressing will keep for a short time if refrigerated. Allow it to return to room temperature before using.

Variations: Add herbs, or very finely chopped vegetables (celery is especially good). A pinch of chilli powder — lovely with a raw cabbage and onion salad (omit the dry mustard for this one).

> 3 tbs smooth peanut butter
> 1 tbs lemon juice
> approx. 1/8 pint (70ml) water
> good pinch dry mustard
> seasoning to taste

Tahini Dressing

4 tbs tahini
4 tbs vegetable oil
2 tbs lemon juice
soya sauce to taste
seasoning to taste
1 tbs chopped parsley
or chives (optional)

In a bowl, stir together all the ingredients, making sure they are well mixed. Adjust the amount of soya sauce and seasoning to suit your own taste. You can also make the dressing thinner if necessary by adding a drop more oil, lemon juice or water. Stir in the parsley or chives to give colour.

Store this dressing in the fridge, but it's best used within a few days.

Variations: Add chopped garlic or a pinch of garlic salt — not too much or you'll lose the subtle sesame-like taste. Paprika goes well too.

The Packed Lunch

If you're vegan, you may well find you have to take a packed lunch to work or place of study — either that or go hungry. Although it's well worth encouraging canteens and restaurants to provide vegan dishes on their menus, a packed lunch will keep down costs, allow you to get away from the building (to have a picnic when the weather is right, for example), and free you to enjoy the foods you like best even when you're away from home.

It also means, of course, someone has to plan and prepare it!

Sandwiches are the obvious choice. Make them with wholemeal bread, use a shop-bought spread or pâté, or — better still — make your own. Add lots of salad and a piece of fresh fruit or cake and you're all set. (Although sandwiches are best made in the morning, they can be put together the night before, wrapped well, and kept in the fridge overnight.) A simpler idea is to keep crispbread or savoury biscuits in your desk or locker, and to take a small polythene container of pâté or spread with you each day. Vegetable sticks — carrot, celery, green pepper — are quick to prepare, won't disintegrate in the lunch box, and add a fresh crisp taste to your lunch.

Another idea is to make a habit of making extra pasties, croquettes or savoury flans (you could make an individual tart or turnover when you're putting together a main-course flan). Keep these in fridge or freezer, ready for an instant lunch.

Soya yoghurt can be carried in small plastic cartons, as can salads such as coleslaw (though check that the the tops fit properly!). Nuts and raisins can be added to savoury snacks, or just nibbled as needed. Look out also for the many sweet bars now available in wholefood and health-food shops and made from a wide range of ingredients — including oats, carob chips, coconut and dried apricots. Not only are they packed with nutrients, but they're high in energy value — at a pinch, you could lunch on one of them and still manage to keep going all afternoon.

For winter lunching you might consider investing in a small thermos flask (there are some very slimline ones in the shops these days) and taking hot, home-made soup.

Spreads

Cashew Butter

8 oz (225g) cashew nut pieces
approx. 4 tbs vegetable oil
good pinch of salt

The cashews can be used raw, but have a much better flavour if dry-roasted first. To do this, put them into a heavy-based pan and cook over a medium heat, stirring frequently, until they begin to brown. Let them cool before putting them into a grinder and making a fine powder of them.

Put the powder into a bowl and stir in the oil gradually, making sure it is well mixed. Add just enough to make a thick but not too oily paste. Flavour with salt and store in an airtight jar in the fridge.

Variations: Cashew nut butter can be given a chocolate flavour by adding one or two tablespoons of cocoa (or, better still, carob powder which is far more nutritious!). Add chopped herbs to make a savoury butter. Use the same process to make other nut butters. Roasted hazelnuts and almonds are both very tasty. Peanuts are cheapest. They can be raw, roasted, or a mixture of both. Add some sunflower seeds for an unusual peanut butter. For a lower-fat version mix the ground nuts with water instead of oil.

Put a small amount of bicarbonate of soda into a dish and stand it in your fridge. It will absorb smells.

Avocado Tofu Spread

Halve the avocado and remove the stone. Peel the flesh and then cut it into cubes. Either use a fork to mash together all the ingredients or put them into a blender to make a thick, smooth paste.

Adjust the seasoning to taste. If liked you can chill the spread before serving — a day or so in the fridge will allow the flavour to 'ripen'.

Variations: Use finely chopped garlic or celery instead of the onion, or maybe a sprinkling of herbs. By adding a drop of water and mixing well you can turn this into a dip — great with tortilla or corn chips!

> 1 medium (ripe) avocado
> 8 oz (225g) tofu,
>   well drained
> 2 tbs vegetable oil
> 2 tbs lemon juice
> 1/2 small onion, very
>   finely chopped
> seasoning to taste
> good pinch of chilli
>   powder

Hummus (Chick Pea Spread)

Put the chick peas into a saucepan with fresh water, bring them to a boil and continue fast cooking for 10 minutes. Then lower the heat, cover the pan and cook for 1-11/2 hours, or until the chick peas are tender.

Drain, reserving a little of the water in which the chick peas were cooked, and set aside to cool.

Grind the chick peas to a powder in a grinder (they can also be mashed with a fork, or pounded with a pestle and mortar, but it will take a lot longer, and the result will be a coarser-textured hummus).

> 8 oz (225g) chick peas,
>   soaked overnight
> 4 tbs tahini
> 4 tbs vegetable oil
>   (preferably olive)
> 1-2 cloves garlic, peeled
>   and crushed
> 1-2 lemons
> seasoning to taste
> 1/2-1 tsp paprika

Mix together the ground chickpeas, tahini, vegetable oil and garlic. Add the lemon juice and, if liked, a little of the lemon peel grated very fine. Now pour in just enough of the reserved cooking liquid to make the mixture easy to spread. Season to taste and add the paprika. Chilling it improves the flavour.

If kept in an airtight container in the fridge, hummus will stay fresh for several days.

Variations: Hummus is a favourite Middle Eastern dish, usually eaten with falafels and pita bread. Apart from varying the balance of tahini, oil and lemon juice, there is little you can do to vary it. However, call it Chick Pea Spread and you're free to ring the changes! Stir in some peanut butter instead of tahini. Add curry powder or cumin. Sprinkle with chopped black olives, red pepper and celery. Throw in a handful of fresh mint, chopped fine. (Use pre-cooked or tinned beans and you can make hummus in next to no time.)

Sunflower and Mushroom Spread

4 oz (115g) sunflower seeds
approx. 4 tbs vegetable oil
4 oz (115g) mushrooms, washed and finely chopped
approx. 2 tbs fresh tarragon, parsley or chives
seasoning to taste
garlic salt (optional)

Dry roast the sunflower seeds by putting them into a heavy-based pan and cooking over a medium heat until they begin to brown. Stir them every now and again so that they colour evenly. Grind to a coarse powder.

In another pan, heat two tablespoons of oil and gently fry the mushrooms for a few minutes to soften.

Mix together the ground seeds and

the contents of the mushroom pan (including any remaining liquid), plus the rest of the oil, the herbs and seasoning. Add garlic salt to taste, if you like it.

Store the spread in an airtight container in the fridge.

Variations: Add chopped red or green pepper — either raw or lightly cooked with the mushrooms. Celery goes well too. Vary the herbs. For a smoother-textured spread, mix all the ingredients in a blender. For a chunkier spread, chop rather than grind the seeds.

Sweet Tahini Spread

Simply mash together (or purée in a blender) all the ingredients, except the walnuts. Adjust the sweetness to taste.

Use the spread at once — it really doesn't keep very well. The amount given here is enough for two to three rounds of sandwiches.

A sprinkling of chopped walnuts makes a delicious addition.

> **2 tbs tahini**
> **1 large ripe banana**
> **1/2-1 tbs syrup or maple syrup**
> **squeeze of lemon juice**
> **walnuts (optional)**

Variations: Tahini is very versatile and can be used as a 'binder' for all sorts of spreads. Well-drained apple purée, for example, can be thickened with tahini. So can apple butter. Or mix it with a little orange juice and grated rind (use the thicker tahini from the bottom of the jar for this!). It's also good in savoury spreads.

Wholemeal Bread

2 oz (55g) fresh or 1 oz (30g) dried yeast
1 tsp sugar or molasses
3 lb (1.4Kg) wholemeal flour
approx. 11/2 pints (850ml) lukewarm water
generous pinch of salt

In a small bowl, cream together the yeast, sugar or molasses, and about a quarter of the water, mixing them well so that the yeast and sweetener dissolve. Set the mixture aside in a warm spot for five minutes, or until it starts to froth.

Put the flour into a large bowl and add the yeast and the rest of the water (which should still be lukewarm). Use your hands to mix everything, adding a drop more water if it seems too dry. Knead the dough for a few minutes, then cover the bowl with a clean tea towel and stand it in a warm spot for 15-30 minutes, or until the dough is well risen. Knead it briefly again and then divide it into two, even-sized portions and shape into loaves. Grease two large loaf tins, put in the dough and again leave them in a warm spot until the dough rises to the top of the tins. (The oven is a good place to leave them — set it on the lowest setting; this also means you don't need to move the tins again, which is a good thing as a sharp knock can make the dough deflate.)

Bake at 400°F/200°C/Gas Mark 6 for 20-35 minutes. To test if the bread is cooked tap the bottom of the loaf with your knuckles — when ready it will sound hollow. Cool the loaves on a wire rack (if you put a clean tea towel over them, the centre will be softer). For a crisper crust remove the loaves from the tins and return them to the oven for literally five minutes more before cooling them.

Variations: You can make four small loaves if you prefer — store the extra in fridge or freezer. Or use half the mixture to make wholemeal baps — follow the same procedure but instead of shaping the dough into a second loaf, divide it into 6-8 small pieces (all about the same size), shape them into baps and brush lightly with flour. Place on a greased baking sheet and when they've doubled in size, cook them at the same temperature, but for about 10 minutes only.

Sandwich or Bap Filling Ideas

- Peanut butter, celery, alfalfa sprouts or cress.
- Mashed dates with chopped roasted hazelnuts.
- Left-over beans mashed, flavoured with yeast extract and/or herbs, plus lettuce, cucumber slices.
- Thinly-sliced tinned nut meat with tomato and watercress.
- Tahini, spring onions, chopped olives and/or capers.
- Left-over curry mashed to a paste — add finely sliced raw cabbage.
- Any favourite jam with banana slices and chopped nuts.
- Grated carrots and raisins bound together with soya mayonnaise.
- Mashed or puréed tofu — mixed with tahini, lemon juice, lots of seasoning and fresh parsley.
- Any vegan pâté with raw mushrooms, sliced red pepper.
- Apple butter with raisins, a sprinkling of sunflower seeds.
- Peanut butter on one slice, tahini on the other, mung beans sprouts in the middle.
- Left-over nut or bean bakes — cut into thick slices and topped with chopped Chinese leaves.
- Chestnut purée (from a tin or tube) with desiccated coconut.
- Avocado mashed with finely chopped garlic or pepper, soya mayonnaise to bind, and a few chopped walnuts.
- Spread bread with yeast extract, add mixed salad.
- Cold 'Scrambled Tofu' (see page 13) with slices of tomato.
- Hazelnut butter with thinly-sliced apple or pear.
- Pease pudding (from a tin) with celery, lettuce or pepper.
- Any vegan 'burgers' or 'sausages' — topped with raw onion, ketchup, relish or whatever you fancy!

Cooker-Top Meals

In general, these are relatively quick to prepare — though some (pancakes for example) can be more complicated. They may well require more than one saucepan, and a good sense of timing! The advantage of cooking your meals this way is that as you get everything done there and then, you can control it as you go along, adding more liquid, herbs or whatever as you think necessary. Those with limited cooking facilities may especially like the idea of cooking everything in one pan. And *do* combine things if you want to. Traditional eating habits have instilled in us the idea of a savoury plus side vegetables (including potatoes or a grain such as rice), with everything cooked separately. But there's no reason why you shouldn't stir the vegetables into the savoury, or at least cook them in the same pan. A fold-up steamer that fits into a saucepan is ideal for cooking two things at once — you can boil one vegetable below and steam another on top.

If there's one utensil that particularly lends itself to economical and speedy cooker-top meals, it has to be the wok. Small ones are now available if your cooker is small (or if you're cooking for one only). Woks are so constructed that heat is effectively used for evenly cooked ingredients, they require the minimum of oil for frying (good for your pocket *and* your heart!), and afterwards they come clean like a dream. Don't think you can only use them for stir fries either — they're very adaptable and can be used to cook most foods.

Sweet and Sour 'Pork' with Cashews

5 oz (140g) soya 'pork'
chunks, hydrated in
water

For sauce:

1/3 pint (200ml) water
1 celery stick, finely
chopped
1 red pepper, finely
chopped
1/2 clove garlic, crushed
(or good pinch of garlic
salt)
pinch of ground cloves
seasoning to taste
1 tbs raw cane sugar
1 tbs soya sauce
1 tbs cornflour
a few spoonfuls of orange
or pineapple juice
(optional)
2 oz (55g) cashew nut
pieces

Cover the soya 'pork' chunks with fresh water, bring to the boil and then cook gently for 10 minutes.

Meanwhile, put the water, celery, onion, pepper and garlic into a clean saucepan and bring to the boil. Lower the heat, cover the pan and simmer for 10 minutes.

Pour off any remaining liquid (use fresh if most of it has cooked away) and stir in the cloves, seasoning, sugar, soya sauce and cornflour. Return this to the vegetable mixture and add the soya chunks. Cook gently, stirring frequently, until the sauce thickens and the soya chunks are heated through. You may need to add extra liquid — fruit juice gives a lovely flavour. Stir in the nuts.

Nice with: Wholemeal noodles instead of the usual rice — though that tastes good too.

Variations: The basic sauce can be used to add interest to vegetables, or as a topping for pancakes and stir fries. Or add other ingredients instead of the soya chunks — beans are tasty (and easier to digest than when served unadorned!). Mushrooms and celery go well with Sweet and Sour Sauce (throw in some walnuts for crunch), and nut croquettes or loaf are delicious topped with this sauce. Add chopped pineapple, vary the spices or use wine vinegar instead of lemon juice.

Savoury Pancakes

In a bowl sift together the flours, then gradually whisk in the water to make a light smooth sauce. Add the oil. Cover the bowl and leave in a cool spot for 30 minutes.

Meanwhile, prepare the filling. Chop the spinach into pieces and put into a saucepan with the onions and margarine. Cook gently for 5-10 minutes, stirring occasionally, until the spinach is tender. Drain well. Stir in the nuts. Keep the mixture warm (the best way is on a plate over a pan of hot water – don't forget to cover the top).

To make the white sauce, heat the oil and sprinkle in the flour, then add the milk. Cook gently, stirring continually, until the sauce thickens, then add nutmeg and seasoning. Keep this warm too.

When ready to make the pancakes, whisk the batter again – it should be the consistency of single cream, so add a drop more liquid if it is too thick.

Heat a little oil in a heavy-based pan and make sure it is spread right across the base. When it begins to smoke, pour in just a spoonful or two of the batter, turning the pan so that it spreads evenly. Cook gently until it begins to colour underneath, then use a spatula to turn the pancake (or toss it!) and cook the other side.

Keep the pancakes warm whilst using the rest of the batter in the same way. Fill each one with some of the spinach and peanut mixture, roll them up and top with a little of the sauce. For a more impressive-looking presentation (and a

For pancakes:

4 oz (115g) wholemeal
flour
2 oz (55g) soya flour
approx. 1/2 pint (285ml)
water
2 tsp vegetable oil
vegetable oil for frying

For filling:

1lb (445g) spinach,
washed and trimmed
(or frozen equivalent)
3 spring onions, finely
chopped
1 oz (30g) margarine
2 oz (55g) raw peanuts,
coarsely chopped

For sauce:

2 tbs vegetable oil
1 oz (30g) wholemeal
flour
1/2 pint (285ml) soya
milk
good pinch nutmeg
seasoning to taste
wholemeal breadcrumbs
(optional)

way to make sure the pancakes are piping hot) arrange the filled pancakes side by side in a shallow ovenproof dish, top with the sauce and breadcrumbs, and pop the dish under a hot grill for a few minutes.

Nice with: A red pepper, sweetcorn and beansprout salad. Add warm wholemeal baps for the extra hungry.

Variations: Pancakes made this way can be filled with a wide variety of ingredients. Use any left-over vegetables (curried are super — top the pancakes with soya yoghurt into which you've chopped cucumber and chives). Fry mushrooms and walnuts to use as a stuffing. Mix chopped tofu into ratatouille (use the frozen variety if you've no time to make it), or add it to fried courgettes with sesame seeds. Don't stop at vegetables either — fill your pancakes with a soya 'meat' mixture, left-over bean stew or grain dish. Top with tomato sauce instead of white sauce.

Stock left over from cooked vegetables is full of nutrients. Use it as a base for soups, stews, or to makes sauces. If you don't want to use it at once, vegetable stock can be kept in a screw-top jar in the fridge for several days.

Hawaiian Rice

Cook the rice in boiling water — the time will depend on the kind of rice you use (I like 'quick-cook' Italian rice which, being partly cooked, has much of the goodness sealed in, as well as being ready in no time!). Drain the rice and set aside.

In a clean pan heat the oil and fry the garlic, onion and pepper for a few minutes. Add the celery. Cover the pan and cook for 5-10 minutes, or until the vegetables are just tender. Stir in the well-drained peas and pineapple and leave to heat through.

Flavour with soya sauce and plenty of seasoning. Add a little of the pineapple juice. Serve sprinkled with nuts.

Nice with: A raw cabbage, cucumber and tomato salad.

Variations: Sweet and Sour Sauce (Make your own or buy it in a bottle) could be served with Hawaiian rice. Even easier — thicken the reserved juice with cornflour or arrowroot and add a tablespoon of cider vinegar and a pinch of sugar. Any vegetables can be used. The nuts can be varied — try flaked coconut lightly toasted for a change.

> 8 oz (225g) brown rice
> 2 tbs vegetable oil
> 1 clove garlic, crushed
> 1 medium onion, sliced
> 1 medium red pepper, sliced
> 2 sticks celery, sliced
> 4 oz (115g) cooked peas
> small tin pineapple chunks in natural juice
> soya sauce
> seasoning to taste
> 2 oz (55g) flaked almonds, toasted

> Cook extra rice or pasta, rince through at once with cold water, then drain well. Cover and store in the fridge. You now have the instant making of a salad dish: just add chopped vegetables, nuts and beans, and a tasty dressing. Other grains can be used in the same way.

Winter Stew with Dumplings

1 oz (30g) margarine or 2 tbs vegetable oil
2 leeks, cleaned and chopped
2 carrots, peeled and chopped
2 sticks celery, chopped
1 parsnip, peeled and chopped
1 turnip, peeled and chopped
6 oz (170g) brown lentils, soaked overnight
approx. 3/4 pint (425ml) vegetable stock or water
1 tsp yeast extract
seasoning to taste
1/2 small cabbage, coarsely sliced

For dumplings:

4 oz (115g) self-raising wholemeal flour
1/2 tsp mixed herbs
seasoning to taste
2 oz (55g) vegan 'suet', shredded
1/2 small onion, finely chopped (optional)
cold water to mix
chopped parsley (optional)

Melt the fat in a large pan, add the prepared vegetables (except cabbage), and fry gently for five minutes, stirring occasionally.

Add the drained lentils, vegetable stock, yeast extract and seasoning. Bring the liquid to the boil, then cover the pan and simmer everything for 30 minutes.

To make the dumplings simply mix together the ingredients and add just enough water to make a fairly firm dough. Break this into small pieces (it should make about 12) and shape them into balls.

Add the cabbage to the vegetables and stir well. If necessary, add a drop more liquid to the saucepan and bring to a boil, then drop in the dumplings. Cover the pan again and cook for 15-20 minutes until the vegetables, lentils and dumplings are cooked. Serve hot.

A sprinkling of fresh parsley adds colour. (If you are left with a lot of liquid, either pour off the excess, or mix it with a spoonful of flour, return it to the pan, and cook until the stew thickens.)

Nice with: French bread or wholemeal baps. A watercress salad would balance the meal.

Variations: Any vegetables can be used. For an even more filling stew add soya 'meat' or potatoes. Other pulses could replace the lentils (adjust the cooking time accordingly). Chopped nuts or seeds could be added to the dumplings (caraway seeds, for example).

Deep-Fried Tofu Cutlets

Mix the flour with the seasoning. Add sesame seeds and/or herbs, if used. Dip the tofu cutlets into the mixture making sure they are well coated, then shake lightly to remove any excess flour.

Heat a pan with oil and drop in the cutlets a few at a time (test the oil for temperature first by dropping in some crumbs — it should sizzle when it's ready). Cook the cutlets just long enough for the coating to brown. The inside will still be creamy. Drain the cutlets on paper towels before serving.

Nice with: Vegetables or salad, potatoes or a grain. In fact this simple way of cooking tofu is a great meat substitute when you want to serve a traditional-style meal.

Variations: To give the tofu more flavour, marinate it first (for at least 15 minutes) in soya sauce. Or make a more exotic sauce by mixing soya with some dry sherry, a pinch of sugar and ground ginger. Garlic salt could be used too. Marinating the tofu makes the flavour adhere better.

> **two 10 oz (285g) packets firm tofu**
> **wholemeal flour**
> **seasoning**
> **1 oz (30g) sesame seeds (optional)**
> **herbs (optional)**
> **vegetable oil for frying**

Tofu should be as dry as possible before it is used. Drain it by wrapping it in a clean tea towel and leaving it with a weight (such as a heavy bread board) on top for a short while. If you don't want to use the whole piece store any excess in a jar or dish in the fridge, covered with cold water. Change the water daily and it should stay fresh for up to seven days.

Leek and Tofu Stir-Fry

approx. 2 tbs vegetable
oil
1/2 medium onion,
sliced
1 medium leek, cleaned
and sliced
1 medium carrot, cut
into thin strips
2 oz (55g) mushrooms,
sliced
4 oz (115g) beansprouts
8 oz (225g) tofu, well-
drained and diced
small tin of bamboo
shoots or fresh
watercress

Heat the oil (if using a wok all you need do is brush the surface with oil). Add the onion, leek and carrot and cook over a medium heat, stirring continually, until they begin to soften. Add the mushrooms, stir well, cover the pan and cook for a few minutes more.

Stir in the beansprouts, tofu and sliced bamboo shoots or watercress. Cook for literally a minute or two more, stirring continually, to heat through.

Nice with: Any grain dish — rice is traditional, bulgur is quick, millet is unusual. Have soya sauce at the table.

Variations: Use the filling to stuff pancakes, or in a lasagne. If you don't have the listed vegetables handy, use whatever you do have. Nuts, especially cashews, could replace the tofu.

Cauliflower with Tahini Sauce

1 large cauliflower
1 tbs vegetable oil
1 oz (30g) wholemeal flour
approx. 1/3 pint (220ml)
vegetable stock or water
1-2 tbs tahini
seasoning to taste
3 tomatoes, cut into
quarters
2 oz (55g) wholemeal
breadcrumbs

Divide the cauliflower into florets (as even in size as possible) and boil or steam them for 5-10 minutes until just cooked but not mushy.

Meanwhile, heat the oil and sprinkle in the flour. Cook briefly, then add the vegetable stock or water and bring it to a boil, stirring continually. Stir in tahini to taste and, if the sauce is too thick, adjust the consistency with a drop more liquid. Season to taste.

Put the cauliflower in a ovenproof dish and cover with sauce. Arrange the tomato quarters around the edge. Top with breadcrumbs and put dish under a grill for a few minutes to brown crumbs.

Nice with: Jacket potatoes, new potatoes or chips with a colourful selection of vegetables (such as peas and carrots).

Variations: This quick and easy sauce can be served with a variety of vegetables, nut loaves or burgers. Add chopped parsley for colour.

Chilli Beans

Put the beans into clean water, bring them to a boil and fast boil for 10 minutes, then lower the heat, cover the pan and cook for approximately an hour, or until well cooked. (Use the tinned variety and you'll save a lot of time.)

Meanwhile, heat the oil and lightly fry the onion, garlic and pepper for five minutes. Add the tomatoes, tomato purée and vegetable stock. Stir in the drained kidney beans. Add chilli powder to taste — its strength will depend on the particular brand and how fresh it is, but it can be very fiery, so go slowly at first. Add the sugar, wine vinegar and salt.

Gently simmer the mixture for 10 minutes. Fresh chopped parsley or chives can be added at the last moment for colour and extra flavour.

Nice with: Hot brown rice and a salad — throw in some chopped avocado for an authentic Mexican touch!

> 8 oz (225g) red kidney beans, soaked overnight (or tinned equivalent)
> 2 tbs vegetable oil
> 1 large onion, sliced
> 1 clove garlic, crushed
> 1 green pepper, sliced
> 6 tomatoes, peeled and chopped (or tinned equivalent)
> 3 tbs tomato purée
> approx. 1/3 pint (200ml) vegetable stock
> 1-2 tsp chilli powder
> 1 tbs raw cane sugar
> 1 tbs red wine vinegar
> salt
> parsley or chives (optional)

Spaghetti Napoletana

12 oz (340g) wholemeal
spaghetti

For sauce:

2 tbs vegetable oil
2 spring onions, finely
chopped
1 clove garlic, crushed
1 carrot, finely sliced
1lb (445g) tomatoes,
peeled and chopped
1/2 pint (285ml)
vegetable stock
1/2 tsp thyme
1/2 tsp basil
seasoning to taste
2 oz (55g) sunflower seeds
fresh parsley

Make the sauce first (you can, in fact, make it a day or two in advance and keep it in the fridge). Heat the oil and cook the onions, garlic and carrot for a few minutes, then add the tomatoes and cook a little longer. Stir in the vegetable stock, herbs and seasoning. Bring to the boil then cover the saucepan, lower the heat and cook for 20 minutes. Stir occasionally. You can leave the sauce as it is, or purée the ingredients for a smooth sauce. Add the seeds and chopped parsley.

Bring a large pan of water to the boil and hold the spaghetti in the water. As it softens, curl more of the spaghetti into the pan until it is completely immersed in water. Cook for 10-15 minutes, or until just cooked but still firm (follow cooking time advised on pack).

Drain the cooked spaghetti (wholemeal spaghetti doesn't need to be rinsed in fresh water), put into a serving dish and pour on the sauce. Serve at once.

Nice with: A mixed salad — add nuts or a protein-rich dressing.

Variations: Other pastas can be used instead of spaghetti. The sauce, which is very basic, can be adapted by adding other ingredients instead of the sunflower seeds. Try it with cooked lentils or beans (left-over hummus makes it deliciously creamy). Add mashed tofu. Soya 'minced meat' gives bulk and lots of protein, as well as turning the whole thing into a traditional Spaghetti Bol-

ognaise. Be adventurous with herbs too.
Or try chilli powder instead for a sauce
with a bite!

Dhal with Peppers and Bananas

Put the split peas in fresh water, bring to
a boil and boil for 10 minutes, then lower
the heat and cover the pan. Cook for 30
minutes, or as long as it takes to reduce
the peas to a purée. Drain off excess
liquid.

In a clean pan, heat the oil and fry
the onion, peppers and garlic until they
begin to soften. Add the lemon juice and
spices. Stir to make a paste, and cook a
few minutes more, stirring occasionally.
At the last moment add the bananas.

Nice with: Any grain — millet would
make a change from rice. A fresh, green
salad would make a good contrast. Soya
yoghurt could be spooned over the top —
add grated apple.

Variations: Dhals vary enormously
from one part of India to another. Use
other spices if you like — cloves, cinnamon, ginger and fenugreek are good
choices. Try them in combinations that
appeal to you personally. Dhal benefits
from being made a day or so in advance
and then reheated. Use other split
pulses if you prefer.

> 8 oz (225g) split peas,
>   soaked overnight
> 2 tbs vegetable oil
> 1 onion, chopped
> 1 red pepper, chopped
> 1 green pepper, chopped
> 1 clove garlic, crushed
> 1 tbs lemon juice
> 1/2 tsp turmeric
> 1/2 tsp coriander
> 1/2 tsp ground cumin
> 1/2 tsp paprika
> seasoning to taste
> 2 bananas, peeled and
>   cut into chunks

Brazilian Croquettes

1/2 red pepper,
chopped fine
1 medium onion,
chopped fine
2-3 tbs vegetable oil
1 oz (30g) wholemeal
flour
1/4 pint (140ml)
vegetable stock
1 tbs tomato purée
6 oz (170g) Brazil nuts,
coarsely grated
2 oz (55g) wholemeal
breadcrumbs
1 oz (30g) oats
good pinch of thyme
or oregano
seasoning to taste
extra oats for coating
vegetable oil for frying

Cook the pepper and onion gently in the oil until beginning to soften. Stir in the flour and cook for a minute more.

Pour in the stock, add the tomato purée and stir well — so that the purée dissolves. Bring the liquid to a boil, still stirring frequently, so that the sauce thickens. Remove the pan from the heat.

Mix in the nuts, breadcrumbs, oats, herbs and seasoning, then set the mixture aside for a while so that it firms up. Use your hands to divide the mixture into eight pieces, shape them into croquettes and roll each one firmly in the oats.

Heat a drop of oil and fry the croquettes over a medium heat, turning them frequently so that they are evenly cooked. When the oat coating is crisp and browned, remove the croquettes and drain them on paper towels before serving.

Nice with: Your favourite vegetables (ratatouille goes particularly well) and potatoes or brown rice. Or serve cold with a salad.

When using your hands to shape croquettes, roll out pastry, or whatever, dust them very lightly with flour to stop the mixture or dough sticking to your skin.

Oven-Baked Meals

Baking things in the oven is a perfect method to use when you're entertaining guests. It means you can prepare the main savoury dish beforehand, switch on the heat when everyone arrives, and then go off and relax until the food is ready to be taken to the table.

The perfect accompaniment to such a dish is, of course, a large fresh salad. But you might well feel you'd like something more — in which case choose ingredients that can also be cooked in the oven alongside the main dish. For example, with stuffed vegetables or nut loaf you could cook roast or jacket potatoes. With a lasagne, how about a hot dessert such as fruit pie or crumble? With pasties you could bake some carrots and parsnips, with moussaka do rice (which is delicious cooked in the oven for a change).

Using your oven to the full makes sense for a whole lot of reasons. When you're cooking just one dish, and not preparing a full-scale meal, take the opportunity to roast some nuts (for nut butter), or make granola or a cake. And if you're lucky enough to have a freezer, and smart enough to plan in advance, don't forget the many advantages of preparing and cooking double quantities of the dishes you eat most often and then keeping the extra portion for another day.

Suggested oven temperatures are only a guide, as every oven will differ depending on how new or old, well insulated or efficient it is. The only way to be sure of success is to get used to your own oven by experimenting, and carefully noting the results. You may find that temperatures given here (and in other cookery books) need to be adjusted slightly.

Courgette Lasagne

10 oz (285g) lasagne —
regular or wholewheat
approx. 3 tbs
vegetable oil
1 onion, sliced
1 red pepper, sliced
3 medium courgettes,
sliced
4 oz (115g) sweetcorn —
fresh, frozen or tinned
3 oz (85g) walnuts,
coarsely chopped
seasoning to taste

For sauce:

2tbs vegetable oil
11/2 oz (45g) wholemeal
flour
3/4 pt (425ml) soya milk
seasoning to taste
2oz (55g) wholemeal
breadcrumbs
1oz (30g) margarine
fresh parsley (optional)

Bring a large saucepan of water to the boil and add a teaspoonful of oil (this helps to stop the sheets of pasta sticking together). Drop in the sheets one by one and cook for the time recommended on the packet.

When ready, remove them at once from the heat, drain, put them under cold running water (to halt the cooking process). Put them to one side. The best way to keep them is laid out flat on clean tea towels.

Heat the rest of the oil and cook the onion and pepper together for a few minutes to soften. Add the courgettes, stir, then cover the pan and cook gently until the courgettes begin to soften.

Meanwhile, cook the sweetcorn. Drain it and add to the courgette mixture with the walnuts and seasoning to taste.

Make a white sauce by heating the oil and stirring in the flour. When it begins to colour add the soya milk and mix well to keep it smooth. As it heats it will thicken. Add seasoning.

Lightly grease an ovenproof dish and lay one third of the pasta across the bottom. Top with half the courgette mix and a spoonful or two of the sauce. Repeat this and then finish with the remaining pasta. Pour the rest of the sauce over the top and spread it evenly. Sprinkle the top with breadcrumbs and dot with the margarine. Add lots of chopped parsley, if liked.

Bake at 375ºF/190ºC/Gas Mark 5 for 30 minutes.

46

Nice with: A summer salad — try adding chopped fennel and some olives for a real Italian taste!

Variations: Any fillings can be used instead of the courgettes — the lentil mixture described in Lentil Moussaka, for example, would be ideal. Other nuts could replace the walnuts — or try chopped tofu. Instead of using soya milk for the sauce, make it with water and stir in a spoonful or two of tahini.

Nut Loaf

Heat the oil and cook the onion and celery just long enough to soften. Stir in the tomatoes and cook a minute more.

Now add all the remaining ingredients and mix thoroughly. (The soya flour should be stirred into the vegetable stock first.) Spoon the mixture into a small, lightly-greased loaf tin. Smooth the top.

Bake at 375°F/190°C/Gas Mark 5 for 40-50 minutes, or until firm. Remove carefully from tin and serve hot or cold, cut into slices.

Nice with: Green vegetables, and new or jacket potatoes. Add a tomato sauce or gravy, if liked.

Variations: Use just one kind of nut, or any mixture of nuts and seeds. Add other vegetables — green peppers, mushrooms, sliced olives, whatever you have to hand. The same mixture can be used to stuff vegetables. Omit the soya flour if you're not too worried about a firm-textured loaf.

2tbs vegetable oil
1 large onion, finely chopped
2 sticks celery, finely chopped
4 tomatoes, peeled and chopped
6 oz (170g) mixed nuts, coarsely ground
2 oz (55g) sunflower seeds
4 oz (115g) wholemeal breadcrumbs
1/2 pint (285ml) vegetable stock
1oz (30g) soya flour
1/4 tsp dried sage
1/4 tsp dried rosemary
seasoning to taste

Marrow and Chick Pea Bake

2 tbs vegetable oil
1 onion, chopped
1 medium marrow
14 oz (395g) tin
tomatoes, broken up
14 oz (395g) tin cooked
chick peas
1/2 - 1 tsp dried basil
seasoning to taste
2 medium potatoes
1 oz (30g) margarine

Heat the oil and fry the chopped onion for five minutes.

Cut the marrow into slices about 1" (25mm) thick, peel them and remove the seeds, then cut the flesh into quarters. Add these to the saucepan with the contents of the tin of tomatoes. Cook for five minutes more.

Drain the chick peas and stir them into the first mixture with the basil and seasoning. Transfer everything to a small, lightly-greased casserole and smooth the top. Peel and thinly slice the potatoes and arrange them over the vegetables. Dot with margarine.

Bake at 375°F/190°C/Gas Mark 5 for 40-45 minutes. When the potatoes are cooked, serve at once.

Nice with: A green salad and warm wholemeal baps or French bread.

Variations: Any cooked beans can be used. This mixture is also good in a pie — line a dish with pastry, fill with the marrow and chick pea mixture, and top with more pastry instead of the potato. If making a pie, drain off surplus liquid first.

Peeling vegetables isn't only a time-consuming and fiddly business, it actually means you throw out much of the goodness along with the peel. A much better idea is to scrub the vegetables in water, cutting off only peel that is damaged.

'Sausage' and Bean Hot Pot

Cover the beans with water and bring them to the boil. Continue boiling for ten minutes, then lower the heat, cover the pan and cook gently for 1 1/2-2 hours, or until almost cooked. Add more water if necessary, but drain off the excess once the beans are soft.

Roughly chop the tomatoes and add them to the beans with their juice and the purée.

Heat most of the oil in a clean pan and fry the pepper and onion, stirring occasionally. Add the garlic, if used, and cook a few minutes more. Spoon the vegetables into the beans. Add chilli powder to taste (watch it though — depending on the brand, it can be *very* hot!). Add seasoning.

Fry the sausages in the remaining oil and then stir them into the bean mixture. Chop them into segments if preferred.

Although it could be eaten as it is, this combination benefits from being left in a low oven for a while for the flavours to blend. This means you can prepare it the day before and then heat it up — which also makes it ideal for when you're entertaining.

Nice with: Potatoes — jacket, mashed or boiled. Or fresh bread would be fine, and would save cooking. A watercress salad would make a good balance.

Variations: Any beans could be used instead of haricot, though they are especially good in this dish. It can be made in

1/2 lb (225g) haricot
beans, soaked overnight
14 oz (395g) tin of
tomatoes
2 tbs tomato purée
2-3 tbs vegetable oil
1 green pepper, sliced
1 small onion, sliced
1/2 clove garlic,
crushed (optional)
good pinch of chilli
powder
seasoning to taste
10 oz (285g) tin small
'sausages'
parsley (optional)

49

a fraction of the time if you use tinned beans. No tinned sausages in the house? Make some up from a packet mix, and cook them in the way described. They'll work just as well. And if you think they won't hold their shape, make them into balls instead.

Filled Jacket Potatoes

4 large, even-sized potatoes

For fillings:

1.

1/2 bunch watercress, washed and chopped
1/3 pint (200ml) plain soya yoghurt
seasoning

2.

1 onion, chopped
1/4 small cabbage, shredded
1/4 pint (140ml) vegetable stock
soya 'Smokey Snaps'

3.

2 medium carrots
1/2 tbs vegetable oil
1/2 oz (15g) margarine
1 oz (30g) sunflower seeds
11/2 oz (45g) sultanas

Choose potatoes with a firm, unblemished skin. Scrub them well, pat dry and prick the skin with a fork. (If you have skewers handy, try sticking them through the potatoes lengthways — it will speed up the cooking process.) Put the potatoes straight onto the wire shelves in the oven and bake at 400°F/200°C/Gas Mark 6 for about an hour, or until the flesh gives when pressed. Cut in half to serve.

Towards the end of the cooking time prepare the fillings. (You can stick to just one for a simpler meal, but if you're having guests it might be fun to serve a variety for them to choose from.)

For filling one, simply mix the chopped watercress into the yoghurt and season generously.

For filling two, put the onion and cabbage into a saucepan with the stock and cook, covered, for just five minutes or so to soften. Drain and serve sprinkled with the 'Smokey Snaps'.

For filling three, slice the carrots (or, better still, cut them into thin strips) and cook them gently in a mixture of oil and melted margarine. After five minutes add the seeds and sultanas and cook a few minutes more.

For filling four, heat the oil and fry the onion to soften. Stir in the chopped tomatoes, add the celery, and cook for five minutes more (if it gets too dry add a drop of water or lemon juice). Mash the tofu, stir it into the sauce with the bean sprouts and cook just long enough to heat through. Season to taste.

For filling five, simply put the beans into a saucepan with the pepper, drained sweetcorn and chilli powder and bring to the boil. Then lower the heat, cover the pan, and simmer for five minutes more to cook the pepper and sweetcorn.

Nice with: Jacket potatoes make a meal in themselves if served topped with delicious fillings and accompanied by a large salad. They can, of course, be served with a savoury dish — in which case top with just a knob of margarine, fresh ground pepper and maybe some parsley.

4.

1 tbs vegetable oil
1 small onion,
  finely chopped
3 large tomatoes,
  peeled and chopped
1 stick celery,
  finely chopped
5 oz (140g) tofu,
  well drained
2 tbs bean sprouts
seasoning to taste

5.

14 oz (395g) tin
  baked beans
1 green pepper,
  diced
2 oz (55g) sweetcorn,
  frozen or tinned
1/2 tsp chilli pow-
  der or to taste

Save gas or electricity by making full use of the oven when baking a savoury dish. Serve it with baked potatoes or baked rice (which takes about an hour in a medium oven). Roast some nuts (in a low oven, turning frequently, until coloured to taste) to make nut butters. Make biscuits or a cake.

Stuffed Peppers

4 large peppers
2 spring onions, chopped
3 oz (85g) bulgur, soaked
in boiling water
2 oz (55g) currants
or raisins
2 oz (55g) nuts, coarsely
chopped (pine kernels,
almond or walnuts
are best)
1-2 tbs vegetable oil
seasoning to taste
1/2 tsp mixed spice
(optional)
tahini, white or tomato
sauce to serve
(optional)

Halve the peppers crossways or lengthways, remove the seeds with a sharp knife, then drop the pepper halves into a saucepan of boiling water and cook for literally two minutes. Remove at once, drain well, put under cold running water and drain again. Arrange the pepper halves side by side in a small, lightly-greased ovenproof dish.

In a bowl stir the onions into the drained bulgur and add the currants, nuts, vegetable oil, seasoning and spice. Spoon some of the mixture into each of the pepper halves and press down lightly. Cover the dish (use silver foil if there is no lid) and bake at 400ºF/200ºC/Gas Mark 6 for 15-20 minutes, or until cooked. Serve with hot tahini, white or tomato sauce poured over the top, if liked.

Nice with: New potatoes and a big, crisp fresh salad.

Variations: The stuffing can be varied by using other grains instead of bulgur (left-overs are ideal), or breadcrumbs. Herbs and strong-flavoured vegetables can be included. Use whatever nuts you have handy, or omit them and add instead chopped chick peas or some tofu. Tahini can be stirred in to make the mixture moist (or use vegetable stock). The same fillings can be used with other vegetables instead of peppers — popular examples are onions, tomatoes, thick marrow slices, courgettes and aubergines.

Quick Pizza

Sift together the flour, baking powder, seasoning and herbs. Make a well in the centre of the dry ingredients, pour in the milk and mix thoroughly to make a fairly firm dough. Knead briefly, then divide into four equal pieces and shape into rounds. Place them on lightly-greased baking sheets and press them down to an even depth.

Combine the tomatoes, basil and garlic salt in a small saucepan and bring to the boil. Then lower the heat and simmer until the tomatoes thicken into a sauce. Leave to cool briefly before spreading this over the prepared pizza bases.

Arrange the mushrooms, pepper rings and drained sweetcorn or peas on top of the sauce. Slice the drained artichoke hearts, if used, and divide between the pizzas. Sprinkle with chopped olives and the pumpkin seeds. Trickle a little oil over the top of the ingredients to stop everything drying out in the oven.

Bake at 400°F/200°C/Gas Mark 6 for 20 minutes, or until the dough is cooked.

Nice with: A green salad.

Variations: This is a scone-dough pizza, which is quick to make. Traditionally, pizzas are made with bread dough, which includes yeast and is a more complicated process — though there are plenty of recipes available if you want to try! Be adventurous with your toppings. Start by spreading the base with tomato sauce, then add whatever you like — a variety of vegetables and nuts, chopped

---

8 oz (225g) self-raising wholemeal flour
1 tsp baking powder
seasoning to taste
1-2 tsp mixed herbs
approx. 1/4 pint (140ml) soya milk or water

For topping:

1 14 oz (395g) tin tomatoes
1-2 tsp dried basil
garlic salt
6 oz (170g) mushrooms, thinly sliced
1 large green pepper, cut into rings
3 oz (85g) cooked sweetcorn or peas, drained
1 small tin artichoke hearts (optional)
12 black olives
2 oz (55g) pumpkin seeds
seasoning to taste
vegetable oil

cooked beans (or aduki, which are small to begin with), tofu. If you can't get self-raising wholemeal flour, use plain and add a good two teaspoons of baking powder.

Shepherd's Pie

1 lb (455g) potatoes, peeled and halved
1 oz (30g) margarine
5 oz (140g) soya 'minced meat'
1/2 pint (285ml) vegetable stock
1-2 tsp yeast extract
2 tbs vegetable oil
1 large leek, cleaned and sliced
1 large carrot, peeled and sliced
1 tsp mixed herbs
seasoning to taste
1 oz (30g) wholemeal flour

Steam the potatoes until just soft. Mash them to a thick, smooth purée with half the margarine, then set aside.

Put the soya 'minced meat' into a saucepan with the vegetable stock, bring to a boil and stir in the yeast extract. Simmer gently for 10-15 minutes for the 'minced meat' to hydrate.

Meanwhile, heat the oil and fry the leek and carrot until beginning to soften. Add the herbs, seasoning, and 'minced meat', plus any remaining stock. Bring the mixture to a boil, sprinkle with flour and then lower the heat and cook gently until the mixture thickens and the ingredients are just cooked.

Transfer to an ovenproof dish, and top with the prepared potato, smoothing the surface. Dot with the remaining margarine. Bake at 350°F/180°C/Gas Mark 4 for 30 minutes.

Nice with: All the traditional vegetables — brussels sprouts, carrots, peas. Add warmed crisps if you like, though it shouldn't really be necessary!

Variations: Instead of soya 'minced meat' use lentils in a brown gravy or tomato sauce. Or use a vegetable mixture — maybe with tahini stirred in to thicken it slightly. For a really unusual

Shepherd's Pie, use mashed parsnip instead of potatoes.

Sage and Onion Tart

Sift the flour and salt together, then use your fingertips to rub the margarine into the dry ingredients to make a crumb-like mixture. Add just enough cold water to bind it to a dough, knead very briefly, then cover with clingfilm and leave in a cool spot for 30 minutes.

Heat the oil and fry the chopped onion and pepper to soften. Drain off any excess liquid. Add seasoning and the sunflower seeds.

Mash the tofu with a few tablespoons of cold water, or − better still − use a blender to make the sauce completely smooth. Add sage to taste.

On a floured board, roll out the pastry, then carefully transfer it to line a medium-sized flan dish. (Some people find it easier to roll wholemeal pastry between sheets of clingfilm or polythene − worth a try if you're having problems!) Lay the onion mixture across the base, spreading it evenly. Pour on the tofu sauce. Arrange the onion rings decoratively on top.

Bake at 400°F/200°C/Gas Mark 6 for 30 minutes, or until the pastry is cooked.

Nice with: A hot mixed vegetable dish like ratatouille, with potatoes or rice as a filler. A green salad would go well with it too.

8 oz (225g) wholemeal flour
pinch of salt
4 oz (115g) margarine
2-3 tbs cold water to mix

For filling:

2 tbs vegetable oil
1 lb (455g) onions, chopped very fine (reserve a few rings)
1 red pepper, chopped very fine
seasoning to taste
1 oz (30g) sunflower seeds
10 oz (285g) tofu, well drained
cold water
approx. 1 tsp sage

Variations: Tofu used this way gives a quiche-type filling to a flan. It can be used with all sorts of vegetables — from carrots to courgettes, bean sprouts to beetroot. It's great with fresh (or frozen) asparagus. As tofu is fairly bland to taste, add plenty of seasoning and/or herbs.

Mushroom & Pea Crumble

12 oz (340g) mushrooms, sliced
approx. 3 tbs vegetable oil
1 oz (30g) wholemeal flour
1/2 pint (285ml) vegetable stock or soya milk
seasoning to taste
6 oz (170g) cooked peas, well drained

For crumble:

2 oz (55g) margarine or 3 tbs vegetable oil
4 oz (115g) plain wholemeal flour
1 oz (30g) sesame seeds
1-2 tbs fresh mint, chopped fine
seasoning to taste

Add the mushrooms to one tablespoon of the oil and cook gently, stirring occasionally, for just a few minutes to soften. Drain and set aside.

In a clean pan heat the remaining oil and add the flour. Cook briefly then stir in the stock or soya milk and heat slowly, still stirring, until the sauce begins to thicken. Season to taste, then add the mushrooms and peas.

Put the vegetables into a shallow ovenproof dish. Smooth the top. Make the crumble by rubbing the margarine or oil into the flour to make a mixture like fine breadcrumbs. Stir in the mint and seasoning, and sprinkle over the vegetables. Press the top down lightly.

Bake at 400°F/200°C/Gas Mark 6 for 20 minutes, or until the crumble is cooked and golden.

Nice with: A tomato and watercress salad, and steamed new potatoes.

Variations: This crumble topping can be used with any vegetable combina-

tion. Try it, for example, with the Cauliflower with Tahini Sauce or the vegetables in Courgette Lasagne. Instead of sesame seeds use other finely chopped nuts and vary the herbs.

Lentil Moussaka

If you've time, arrange the aubergine slices on a flat surface, sprinkle lightly with salt and leave for half an hour. They should then be rinsed under cold water and patted dry. (This eliminates any bitter taste.)

Fry the slices gently in 2 tablespoons of the oil, turning when one side begins to colour. When soft, drain the aubergine on a paper towel and set aside.

Cook the lentils in fresh water — they'll take anything from 40-60 minutes. When they're just tender (don't let them get mushy), drain well.

Meanwhile, heat the remaining oil in a clean pan, then cook the onion and pepper for a few minutes. Add the garlic, if used, and cook for a few minutes more. Add the tomatoes — breaking them up as you do so — and the purée. Cook the mixture over a medium heat, stirring frequently, until it becomes a thick sauce. Stir in the lentils, oregano and seasoning.

Lay half the aubergine slices across the base of a greased ovenproof dish. Top with half the lentil mixture. Repeat this to use up the remaining ingredients. Sprinkle breadcrumbs across the top and dot with margarine.

1 large aubergine, sliced thin
4 tbs vegetable oil
8 oz (225g) brown lentils, soaked overnight
1 medium onion, chopped
1 green pepper, chopped
1 clove garlic, crushed (optional)
14 oz (395g) tin tomatoes
2 tbs tomato purée
1-2 tsp oregano
seasoning to taste
2 oz (55g) wholemeal breadcrumbs
1 oz (30g) margarine
parsley (optional)

Bake at 350°F/180°C/Gas Mark 4
for 30 minutes. Serve hot. Fresh parsley sprinkled over the moussaka looks
attractive.

Nice with: Brown rice and a green
salad. Pita bread is also good with
moussaka.

Variations: Use soya 'minced meat'
instead of the lentils. Or mix together
coarsely ground nuts and breadcrumbs
and layer the mixture between the
aubergine slices — adding a generous
amount of herbs. Tofu can also be
mashed and used in moussaka.

Desserts

Because veganism has long (too long!) been associated with self-denial, desserts have tended to be an overlooked element of a vegan diet. Fresh fruit — undoubtedly good for all of us — has been suggested time and again for those who feel the need for something sweet at the end of a meal.

In fact, there are countless desserts that can be made without using animal products. Apart from the very many already on menus in even heavily meat-orientated restaurants, there are more that can be made using readily available 'alternative' ingredients — these include soya milks, creams and yoghurts, agar-agar (instead of gelatine), and vegetable 'suets'.

So, if you have a sweet tooth and crave to indulge it — go right ahead. (You'll go a long way towards convincing your carnivore friends that a vegan diet isn't just something to be endured, but something which can actually be *enjoyed*.) Use dried fruits, nuts, spices, tofu, wholegrains and raw cane sugar and you'll be doing something more — you'll be putting nutrition back into the one course that's too often based on nothing more than white sugar, pre-servatives and colouring. And as we all eat to be nourished, there's nothing wrong with that! I confess to once having had just fruit crumble for my evening meal — it was made with apples from the garden, oats and raw cane sugar, and I topped it with soya yoghurt. Delicious! And a whole lot healthier than most TV dinners!

Stuffed Baked Apples

4 medium-sized cooking
apples
2 tbs cake crumbs
(an ideal way to use
up stale cake)
approx. 2 tbs tahini
approx. 1 tbs raw cane
sugar or syrup
1 oz (30g) chopped
roasted hazelnuts
2 oz (55g) candied peel
1 tsp mixed spice

Use a small and very sharp knife to carefully cut out the core from each of the apples (leaving a large hole right through, into which you can put the stuffing). Also cut a circle round the centre of each apple, just breaking the skin, so that they don't burst during cooking.

Stand the apples close together in a small ovenproof dish.

Mix the breadcrumbs with the tahini, sweetener, chopped nuts, candied peel and spice — the result should be fairly moist, so add extra tahini or syrup if necessary.

Stuff the mixture into the apples — any extra can be piled on top. Pour just an inch or two of water into the dish so that the apples are standing in it. Cover the dish with a lid or silver foil, and bake at 350°F/180°C/Gas Mark 4 for 30 minutes, or until the apples are just cooked. Eat them hot or cold.

Nice with: A nut cream — such as cashew, made by mixing ground cashew nuts with soya milk (preferably concentrated).

Variations: Stale bread or biscuit crumbs can be used, and dried fruit such as raisins or chopped apricots can replace the candied peel (or try fresh grated orange or lemon peel). Instead of a sweetener, the mixture can be moistened with undiluted fruit juice — apple gives a gorgeous flavour.

Blackberry Fool

If using fresh blackberries, wash and drain well. If using frozen, defrost them, then drain well.

Mash or blend the fruit to make a thick purée. Stir in the apple juice or liqueur. Those with a sweet tooth can add sugar to taste — this mixes in best if you powder it in a grinder. Stir together the purée and yoghurt and chill briefly. Adjust the sweetness if necessary.

Serve in individual bowls or glasses topped with a sprinkling of granola.

Variations: Any fruit purée can be used in this recipe. For example: strawberries (use orange juice instead of apple), rhubarb, apricot, blackcurrant and apple, and so on. It's a good way to stretch a small amount of purée so that it serves more people. Nuts make a nice alternative topping to granola.

> 1 lb (455g) fresh or frozen blackberries
> 2 tbs concentrated apple juice or your favourite liqueur
> raw cane sugar to sweeten (optional)
> approx. 2/3 pint (340ml) plain soya yoghurt
> crunchy granola for topping

Blackcurrant 'Ice Cream'

In a blender combine the tofu and fruit juice to make a thick, smooth purée. Use the juice diluted for a less sweet 'ice cream', or undiluted if you have a sweet tooth.

Put the mixture into a freezing tray and place it in the freezer (with the thermostat on the coldest setting). When it begins to freeze, whisk it to break up the

> 1 lb (455g) tofu, well drained
> 1/2 pint (285ml) blackcurrant juice
> a few fresh blackberries (optional)

lumps, then re-freeze. Turn the freezer setting back to normal. Take the 'ice cream' out half an hour or so before you intend to use it — but don't let it go too soft!

Serve in scoops — nice topped with fresh blackberries.

Coconut Tofu Pie

For base:

1/2 lb (225g) vegan digestive biscuits
4 oz (115g) margarine, melted

For filling:

2 large ripe bananas
1 lb (450g) tofu
2 tsp vanilla essence
4 tbs syrup
1/4 pint (140ml) coconut milk*
2 tsp agar-agar

Make the pie base by crushing the biscuits to fine crumbs and mixing them with the melted margarine. Standing a flan ring on top of a baking sheet, then use your fingertips to firmly press the crumbs evenly across the base and up the sides.

In a large bowl mix together the well-mashed bananas, the crumbled tofu, vanilla essence and syrup. Better still, use a blender to make a really smooth purée.

Put the coconut milk into a small saucepan, heat gently, and then sprinkle in the agar-agar. Stir well — so that the agar-agar dissolves — and then boil the mixture for just a minute or two.

Add the coconut milk to the first mixture and stir well. Pour the lot into the prepared base and smooth the top. Leave it to cool, then chill the pie in the fridge so that it sets firm. When ready, lift off the flan ring carefully and serve the pie cut into wedges.

Nice with: A fruit purée on top, or maybe fresh fruit salad. (It's also delicious on its own.)

*Coconut milk can be made from creamed coconut — buy it in a chunk, grate it, add hot water and stir well. Or pour boiling water onto desiccated coconut — you'll need about 4 oz (115g) coconut to 1/4 pint (140ml) water. Allow to soak, then drain well.

Spiced Dried Fruit Crumble

Use a packet of mixed dried fruit, or make up your own combination. If soaked in hot water the fruit should be soft enough to use. Put it into a shallow ovenproof dish and stir in the chopped pineapple (if using the tinned variety, also add a spoonful or two of the juice).

Put the flour into a separate bowl and sprinkle with the cinnamon. Use fingertips to rub the margarine mixture into the flour, breaking up the fat so that the result is a mixture like fine breadcrumbs.

Stir in the oats and sprinkle this evenly over the fruit. Press down the top lightly.

Bake at 375°F/190°C/Gas Mark 5 for 30-35 minutes, or until the topping is crisp and golden. Serve hot or cold.

Nice with: Custard, nut cream, concentrated soya milk.

Variations: Any stewed fruit can be used instead of the dried fruit in this recipe. Add desiccated coconut to the crumble topping for a change. Those with a really sweet tooth might like to add a spoonful of sugar to the crumble.

> 1/2 lb (225g) mixed dried fruits, soaked overnight
> small tin pineapple or fresh equivalent
>
> *For topping:*
>
> 3 oz (85g) wholemeal flour
> 1/2-1 tsp ground cinnamon
> 2 oz (55g) margarine
> 2 oz (55g) oat flakes

Special-Occasion Trifle

6 oz (170g) vegan ginger
biscuits
2 medium bananas
1 packet agar-agar
raspberry jelly
1/3 pint (200ml) thick
custard, made with
packet mix and soya
milk
2 oz (55g) flaked,
roasted almonds
plain chocolate, glacé
cherries, angelica, etc
(optional)

Coarsely crush the biscuits, slice the bananas, make up the jelly according to instructions on pack.

In an attractive medium-sized bowl arrange a layer of half the biscuit crumbs, top with half the bananas, then repeat to use up these two ingredients. Pour on the jelly and leave to set.

Spoon the custard over the jelly, smooth the top, and leave the trifle in a cool spot until needed.

Sprinkle with the flaked almonds. For an even more special trifle, decorate with grated chocolate, glacé cherries and angelica.

Variations: All the above ingredients are available in vegan versions — check the current edition of *The Cruelty-Free Shopper.* Ring the changes by using different biscuits (or sponge cakes), different fruit, other flavours of jelly. Blancmange could replace the custard.

Lemon Ice

1 pint (570ml) water
1 tbs grated lemon rind
1/3 pint (200ml) lemon
juice
syrup to taste

Heat the water, then add the lemon rind and juice, and syrup to taste — not too much as lemon ice is meant to have a sharp flavour. Bring the mixture to a boil and stir continually so that the syrup melts.

Leave on one side to cool.

Meanwhile, set the control on your

freezer to fast-freeze. Pour the lemon mixture into a freezing tray, freeze until firm, then tip it into a bowl and beat to a thick mush (using an electric mixer or egg whisk). Re-freeze. This gives the lemon ice a lighter, lump-free texture. The freezer temperature can now be returned to normal.

Remove the lemon ice from the freezer a short time before you intend to eat it. If the weather is very warm, leave it in the fridge rather than at room temperature — you want it to be soft enough to eat, but not reduced to liquid.

Variations: Try the same recipe using oranges. Other fruit juices or purées can be frozen in this way too — ideal when they are extra cheap. Strawberry ice is especially good. If there are children in the house, make ice lollies by freezing the mixture in moulds.

Dried fruit should preferably be soaked before use, especially the larger varieties. First wash it well, then put it into a bowl with hot or cold water and leave for at least a few hours. Even nicer, soak the fruit in juices such as oranges, apple, grape — maybe adding a drop of sherry, spirits or liqueur. Spices such as cinnamon and ginger could be added during cooking, and lemon juice (and some of the chopped peel) is delicious with all dried fruits. Or for a more exotic flavour, how about orange flower or rose water?

Carrot Cake with Iced Topping

6 oz (170g) wholemeal
flour
1 heaped tsp baking
powder
1/2-1 tsp cinnamon
2 oz (55g) margarine
2 oz (55g) ground
almonds
2-3 oz (55-85g) raw cane
sugar
6 oz (170g) carrots,
peeled and finely grated
1 lemon
approx. 3 tbs orange
juice
2 oz (55g) walnuts,
coarsely chopped
2 oz (55g) raisins

For topping:

1 oz (30g) hard
margarine
3 oz (85g) raw cane
sugar, powdered in
grinder
a little concentrated
soya milk

Stir together the flour, baking powder and cinnamon. Use your fingertips to rub the margarine into the flour to make a crumb-like mixture — make sure there are no large lumps of fat left.

Use a spoon to mix in the ground almonds, sugar and carrots. Add about one tablespoon of finely grated lemon peel.

In a small bowl stir together the juice of the lemon, plus the orange juice. Add this to the flour, making sure that it is well blended. Stir in the nuts and raisins, add the carrot mixture. The dough should be heavy but moist, so add more liquid if necessary. Tip or spoon it into a shallow, medium-sized oblong tin — grease this lightly first.

Bake the cake at 325°F/170°C/Gas Mark 3 for 30-45 minutes, or until it feels cooked but spongey when pressed with your finger. Set aside on a wire rack to cool.

Make the topping by creaming together the margarine, sugar, and just enough milk to bind everything (start with hardly more than a teaspoon of milk and mix well).

Spread the topping evenly over the cake, then leave to set. Cut into squares to serve.

Tea Time Treats

Biscuits, cakes and sweet snacks are things we tend to associate with tea time, though there's no reason why they shouldn't be eaten at other times of day. Scones make a quick and filling breakfast (maybe warmed up in the oven and spread with nut butter). Biscuits are a great late-night snack — it's said that having just a small amount of food and a warm drink before bed helps you sleep better. As an alternative to desserts, cakes can be quick to prepare and delicious to eat (especially if served with fruit purée or concentrated soya milk). Home-made sweets can be popped into a lunch box — if it's a child's lunch box the desire to spend valuable pocket money on commercial sweets will hopefully be lessened!

As with all the food that forms part of your daily eating pattern, base your baking on good and wholesome ingredients. This does mean, of course, that your cakes and biscuits won't stay fresh for as long as the shop-bought varieties — but does that matter? Will they get much chance, anyway, when they come out of the oven smelling so irresistible? Choose the simpler recipes and you'll be able to throw together a batch of biscuits or cakes in no time — a very useful talent when the cupboard seems always to be bare, or when hungry friends have a habit of dropping in unexpectedly. And if you don't have the exact ingredients listed in a recipe — be adventurous. Try alternatives. The recipes in this book are meant to be guidelines, not strict instructions to be adhered to at all costs! If something goes wrong and you end up with a plate of crumbs — treat it as a chance to be creative! Serve them with soya yoghurt, use them as a crumble topping or to stuff apples. Whatever you do with them, they'll taste great.

Ginger Biscuits

1-2 tsp ground ginger
8 oz (225g) plain
wholemeal flour
1 tbs baking powder
pinch of salt
4 tbs syrup
4 oz (115g) raw cane
sugar
3 oz (85g) margarine
1 lemon

Stir together the ginger, flour, baking powder and salt.

In a small saucepan heat the syrup with the sugar and margarine, stirring continually until everything dissolves and is well blended. Add about a tablespoon of lemon juice.

Finely grate a tablespoon of lemon peel. Mix this into the dry ingredients with the syrup and margarine. Stir well to make a stiff dough. Set aside to cool slightly.

On a floured board roll the dough out to about 1/4" (6mm) in thickness. Use a biscuit cutter or glass to cut into rounds. Arrange them on a lightly greased baking sheet and cook at 375°F/190°C/Gas Mark 5 for 10-15 minutes. Carefully transfer them to a wire rack to cool and firm up.

Store in an airtight container when completely cold.

Coconut Flapjacks

4 oz (115g) margarine
4 oz (115g) rolled oats
3 oz (85g) desiccated
coconut
2 oz (55g) raw cane
sugar
1/2-1 tsp ground
nutmeg

Melt the margarine, then add all the other ingredients, mixing well. Grease and flour a small sandwich or Swiss roll tin. Spoon in the oat mixture, then press it down evenly and firmly.

Bake at 350°F/180°C/Gas Mark 4 for about 20 minutes. Check after 15 minutes — if the flapjacks are too brown lower the heat. They are ready when golden and firm to touch.

Cut into squares, then set aside for

short while. When they begin to harden, remove them carefully from the tin and leave on a wire rack to get completely cold before storing.

Variations: A mixture of margarine, oats and sugar makes the basic flapjack. It can be varied by using some syrup or malt instead of all the sugar, by adding other spices, by mixing in a little flour or wheatgerm. Try also stirring in finely chopped dried fruits, such as dates or apricots. Pumpkin or sunflower seeds, chopped peanuts or other nuts make interesting additions. At Christmas add mincemeat.

Date and Walnut Scones

Sift together the flour, baking powder and salt.

Use your fingertips to rub the margarine so that you end up with a mixture like fine breadcrumbs. Add the sugar, dates and nuts.

Now stir in just enough milk to make a soft dough. Roll this out, on a floured board, to a thickness of about 1/2" (15mm). Use a cutter or glass to cut into rounds.

Arrange on an ungreased baking sheet and bake at 450ºF/230ºC/Gas Mark 8 for about 10 minutes. Scones are cooked when firm to touch.

Place on a wire rack to cool completely if you intend to keep them, though scones are especially good eaten whilst still warm — spread them with jam for a real treat.

> 8 oz (225g) plain wholemeal flour
> 4 tsp baking powder
> pinch of salt
> 2 oz (55g) margarine
> 1 oz (30g) raw cane sugar
> 2 oz (55g) dates, coarsely chopped
> 2 oz (55g) walnuts, coarsely chopped
> soya milk to mix

Variations: You can add anything to plain scone dough — any fruits, nuts or seeds; finely grated orange or lemon rind (use fruit juice instead of soya milk); herbs for savoury scones. Molasses instead of sugar will give your scones a treacley taste.

Spiced Apple Cake

4 oz (115g) margarine
4 oz (115g) raw cane sugar
2 oz (55g) sultanas
2 oz (55g) raisins
2 oz (55g) mixed nuts, coarsely chopped
2 tsp bicarbonate of soda
1 tbs boiling water
1/3 pint (200ml) apple purée
8 oz (225g) plain wholemeal flour
1/2-1 tsp cinnamon
1/2 tsp mixed spices

Use a fork to cream together the softened margarine and sugar. Stir in the dried fruit and most of the nuts.

In a separate bowl dissolve the bicarbonate of soda in the boiling water. Add this to the first mixture with the cold apple purée.

Sift together the flour and spices and combine with the other ingredients. The dough should be heavy and moist — if necessary, add a drop more liquid (fruit juice is ideal — especially apple, of course). Spoon the mixture into a medium-sized greased cake tin, smooth the top and sprinkle with remaining nuts (or add them half way through cooking time).

Bake at 350°F/180°C/Gas Mark 4 for approximately an hour. To tell if cake is cooked, stick a small sharp knife into the centre. It should come out dry — so if it seems sticky, cook the cake a little longer.

Leave to cool for a few minutes before carefully removing from the tin and standing on a wire rack.

Variations: Instead of dried fruit use chopped lemon or orange peel (dissolve

the soda in the appropriate juice instead of water). Candied peel also goes well in Spiced Apple Cake. (The apple purée can be left over from a previous meal or, if you're absolutely stuck, from a tin. Make up extra when apples are plentiful and keep some in the fridge or freezer.)

Chocolate Cake

In a bowl cream together the margarine, sugar and syrup.

In another bowl, stir the bicarbonate of soda into the orange juice so that it dissolves. Add to the first mixture.

Sift together the flour, baking powder, cocoa and salt. Gradually stir the dry ingredients into the moist mixture. Add the peel and make sure it is evenly distributed.

Spoon the mixture into a medium-sized greased square tin and smooth the top. Sprinkle generously with sugar — when cooked this gives a crunchy texture to the top of the cake.

Bake at 350°F/180°C/Gas Mark 4 for about 20 minutes. Insert a small sharp knife into the cake to see if it is cooked — it will come out clean when ready. Cool briefly in the tin, then transfer carefully to a wire rack to get completely cold.

Serve cut into squares or slices.

Variations: Instead of orange juice use soya milk. Instead of the orange peel use candied peel, or nuts — coarsely chopped roasted hazelnuts are perfect with chocolate cake.

4 oz (115g) margarine
4 oz (115g) raw cane sugar
1 tbs syrup
1 tsp bicarbonate of soda
1/3 pint (200ml) orange juice
8 oz (225g) plain wholemeal flour
1 tbs baking powder
2 tbs cocoa
pinch of salt
1 tbs orange peel, finely grated
extra raw cane sugar for topping

Mince Pies

6 oz (170g) plain
wholemeal flour
1 tsp baking powder
2 tbs vegetable oil
cold water to mix
12 oz (340g) jar vegan
mincemeat

Make the pastry, if possible, an hour or two before you intend to use it. Do this by sifting the flour and baking powder into a bowl, sprinkling with the oil, then adding just enough cold water to bind the dough together. Knead this briefly, then cover with polythene and chill until needed.

Roll the pastry out on a floured board and use a cutter or glass to cut two thirds of the pastry into rounds. Use these to line small plain or fluted tins, and fill each one with a generous amount of mincemeat. Use a small cutter to make tops and place them over the mincemeat, dampening the edges of the dough with water and pressing together to seal. Prick the tops of the pies with a fork.

Bake at 375°F/190°C/Gas Mark 5 for 20 minutes, or until the pastry is cooked. Serve hot, warm or cold.

Variations: If you don't have a tray of small individual tins, use most of the pastry to cover the base and sides of a pie tin or dish, fill with mincemeat, make a topping and serve the pie cut into wedges. Any fruit filling can be used instead of the mincemeat; a mixture of summer fruits is good, or use apple and blackberries later in the year.

Instant Sweets

Mash all the ingredients so that they stick together (if necessary you could add a tiny amount of fruit juice). Break into small pieces and shape into balls. Roll them in the wheatgerm or carob powder and set aside in the cold for a while before eating.

> **2 oz (55g) ground almonds**
> **2 oz (55g) figs, finely chopped or minced**
> **2 oz (55g) dried apricots, finely chopped or minced**
> **wheatgerm or carob powder to coat**

Mix together the sesame seeds and soya flour. Use a couple of spoonfuls of syrup or malt extract to bind the dry ingredients together, making sure you mix them well.

Turn the mixture into a shallow greased tin and set aside for a while. Serve cut into squares.

> **2 oz (55g) sesame seeds**
> **2 oz (55g) soya flour**
> **syrup or malt extract**

Stir together the tahini and syrup, then add enough crumbs to make a firm dough-like mixture. Add spice if you like it. Break the mixture into even-sized pieces, shape into balls, and roll them in the coconut. Set aside for a short while to firm up.

> **4 tbs tahini**
> **3 tbs syrup**
> **approx. 2 oz (55g) cake or biscuit crumbs**
> **1-2 tsp mixed spice (optional)**
> **desiccated coconut**

Index of Recipes